C000020904

Your Towns and Cities in the

Leicester

in the Great War

THE CALL

Rise, men, rise, be done with slumber,
Gather every quickened nerve;
Great your tasks and great their number;
Will you serve?

Burn, men, burn, until God's fires
Body, soul and spirit claim;
Burn till purpose, thoughts, desires,
Make one flame.

Fight, men, fight, God's clarions call you,
Jesus waits your gleaming sword,
Let not battlefields appal you;
He is Lord.

Hope, men, hope, earth's loads will lighten,
And the rest of Christ be given!
Hope, for God's own dawn must brighten
Into Heaven.

Rev. J.H. Saxton, Leicester, 1914

Your Towns and Cities in the Great War

Leicester
in the Great War

Matthew Richardson

Pen & Sword
MILITARY

First published in Great Britain in 2014 by
PEN & SWORD MILITARY
an imprint of
Pen and Sword Books Ltd
47 Church Street
Barnsley
South Yorkshire S70 2AS

ISBN 978 1 78303 289 1

A CIP record for this book is available from the British Library

Printed and bound in England
by CPI Group (UK) Ltd, Croydon, CR0 4YY

Typeset in Times New Roman by Chic Graphics

Pen & Sword Books Ltd incorporates the imprints of
Pen & Sword Archaeology, Atlas, Aviation, Battleground, Discovery,
Family History, History, Maritime, Military, Naval, Politics, Railways,
Select, Social History, Transport, True Crime, and Claymore Press,
Frontline Books, Leo Cooper, Praetorian Press, Remember When,
Seaforth Publishing and Wharncliffe.

For a complete list of Pen and Sword titles please contact
Pen and Sword Books Limited
47 Church Street, Barnsley, South Yorkshire, S70 2AS, England
E-mail: enquiries@pen-and-sword.co.uk
Website: www.pen-and-sword.co.uk

Contents

Acknowledgements

No work of this nature could ever reach print without the help of an enormous number of people; I am fortunate in that during almost thirty years of research into Leicestershire and its soldiers, I have received tremendous help from numerous people – many of whom were previously strangers – who trusted me with precious family photos and documents to copy, and sometimes even to keep. I thank them all warmly and I ask their forgiveness if, over the passage of time, I have forgotten some of their names.

In relation to this particular book, I wish to thank especially the family of the late Jack Horner, who entrusted to me his wonderful photographs and personal papers. Other individuals without whom I could not have completed this project include Graham Stevenson, Colin Hyde at East Midlands Oral History Archive, and Colonel Terry Cave. Jenny Murray at Shetland Museum Service was especially helpful in relation to Nellie Gilbertson. Joyce Billings, Tony Walne, Ann Jessop, Alison Coates, Ray Scroby, Graham Gilliver and Derek Fussell all provided valuable new information about family members. Gillian Lighton similarly provided marvellous material, both relating to her own family and to the Leicester Secular Society. I am indebted also to Professor Richard Hyman, historian of the Workers' Union, for permission to use his research material, whilst the staff of the Modern Records Centre at the University of Warwick, which holds these papers, were also most helpful. Matt Allen was generous in sharing his photographs, as was Jim Briggs. Margaret Maclean in the Special Collections department of the David Wilson Library at the University of Leicester assisted me with research, as did Robin Jenkins at the Record Office for Leicester, Leicestershire and Rutland, to whom I owe a great deal. I thank him warmly for his support over the years.

My former colleague, Richard Davies, at the Special Collections department of the University of Leeds, as ever was a great help. Ned Newitt deserves special thanks for sharing his marvellous collection of photographs with me (more of Ned's material and his meticulous research can be found on his website, *Who's Who of Radical Leicester*). The editor and staff of the Leicester Mercury (in particular Austin Ruddy) deserve special thanks for making available to me a number of photographs from their archives. The Leicester and Rutland Family History Society kindly publicised my appeal for information, as did the Leicester branch of the Western Front Association. In Wigston, Mark Gamble deserves my heartfelt gratitude for his invaluable assistance with research. As so often before, my parents devoted much time to helping me locate obscure texts, without which this book would have been so much the poorer. Lastly, as always, I thank my long suffering wife Natalia and our children for their forbearance whilst I was at times so obviously distracted by this book from the more important things in life.

I also feel privileged in that in the 1980s I was able to meet some of the last of the generation who lived through the First World War. My interest in the subject at that time was only just developing, but seeking out and meeting those who had actually been involved was both humbling and inspiring. I wish to close by paying tribute to those men and women of the 1914-18 generation, who endured so much in so many different ways during those years, and who for better or worse shaped the world we know today.

Matthew Richardson,
Douglas, 2013

Introduction

Relatively little has been written about Leicester in the Great War from a personal perspective. F.P. Armitage's *Leicester 1914-1918*, though perhaps the 'standard' work, cannot be considered an eye-witness account, because the author did not move to the town until after the war. Likewise, Ben Beazley's *Leicester During The Great War,* whilst offering fairly comprehensive coverage (and indeed considerable detail in some areas), lacks the punch of contemporary accounts. Beazley, however is not to be blamed for this, for such accounts are extremely hard to come by. Leicester people it seems were rather reticent when it came to recording their experiences of war for posterity. Nevertheless, the book which you are about to read differs from its two illustrious predecessors in that, through the assistance of libraries and archives holding unpublished or long out of print accounts, it seeks to document the First World War as it was experienced by Leicester people, both at home and on the battlefields, as far as is possible in their own words.

The more I have studied the First World War over the past thirty years, the more I have come to understand what a complex and multi-faceted thing British experience of that war really was. It was with a kaleidoscope of views and opinions that Britons responded to the world's first global conflict. Indeed, Leicester was richer in this respect than many other towns and cities, the radicalism of its politics at home being matched by the bravery of its soldiers on the battlefield. I hope that in this book I have gone at least some way towards reflecting that diversity of opinion.

Leicester in the last years of the nineteenth century was a prosperous town. It boasted an impressive range of industries, though the emphasis was heavily towards engineering, textiles and, most significantly, footwear. In the period between 1860 and 1914 the hosiery industry

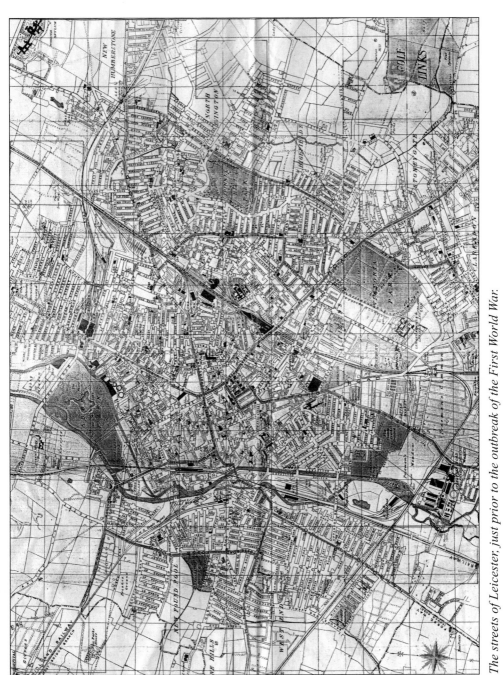

The streets of Leicester, just prior to the outbreak of the First World War.

lost its predominant position in Leicester's economic life, and in terms of numbers employed the boot and shoe industry became the most important in the town. In 1911, 15,727 people were employed in hosiery, and 23,495 in footwear. Engineering, Leicester's third industry, employed 6,162. An important factor contributing to the prosperity of the town was the complementary nature of the labour requirements in the main industries. The hosiery industry had come to employ many more women than men; whilst in footwear the reverse was true, and the engineering industry employed almost exclusively men.

The better off among its 228,000 people lived in the leafy suburbs being developed on the outskirts of the borough, for example along London Road. At the other end of the social spectrum, the poor lived in courts – open squares of dwellings (often tenements) set back from the street - or in what the borough medical officer Dr Killick Millard described as:

> … much old cottage property in need of overhauling and putting into repair [some] considered to be so dangerous or injurious to health as to be unfit for human habitation.[1]

However, the majority of the working and lower middle classes lived in the long straight rows of neat red brick terraced houses, which had sprung up in the last decades of Queen Victoria's reign.

Politically, Leicester had always been Liberal, but the ten years prior to the First World War had seen socialism make steady progress. The town was a stronghold of the Independent Labour Party, and in 1910 played host to the National Peace Conference, confirming that the radical tendency that stretched back to the days of Chartism was still present there.

The First World War presented many challenges to, and placed great strain upon, British society and its liberal traditions. How, for example, could the British government curtail freedom of speech in the interests of furthering the war effort, when it was claimed that the war was being fought precisely to safeguard such freedoms. In many respects, Leicester, with its conflicts and contradictions, represents urban Britain in microcosm between 1914 and 1918.

CHAPTER 1

What will be the end of it all?

International tensions had simmered for years in Europe, and rivalry between Britain and Germany (expressed most openly in a naval arms race) meant that it was really a question of when rather than if a war would break out between them. Yet it was an event in faraway Bosnia which provided the catalyst for war. The assassination of the Austrian Archduke Franz Ferdinand on 28 June 1914 triggered the mobilization of the mighty continental armies of Austria-Hungary, Russia, Germany and France less than one month later, but Britain was not yet in the conflict. As she havered between peace and war, the news of the outbreak of fighting on the continent was not greeted with universal acclaim in Leicester, as it was in some parts of Europe. Instead, at a meeting called by the Leicester Trades Council (the body representing trades unions in the town) on 2 August 1914, several speakers declared that war with Germany would be an utter disaster for Britain and called for her to remain neutral. George Banton of the Independent Labour Party asked the audience:

George Banton, who did much to establish the Labour Party in Leicester in the early twentieth century. He stood for Leicester East in the December 1918 election, but was heavily defeated because of his support for Ramsay MacDonald.
(Courtesy of Ned Newitt)

Is the body of the Archduke worth more than the body of the common ordinary soldier? Are we to go to war with Germany, that advancing and progressive civilization, that people whom, in many ways, England is humbly following up, to help Russia, who means to stamp out those things which make for the liberty of the people?[1]

Ramsay MacDonald, Leicester's Labour MP in 1914. He later became Labour's first ever Prime Minister in 1924.

One of the two Members of Parliament representing Leicester at this time was Ramsay MacDonald, the leader of the Labour Party (not to be confused with the Independent Labour Party, which co-existed alongside it but which maintained stricter socialist policies). The party had strong anti-war traditions, and when the Foreign Secretary made a statement in the House of Commons on 3 August 1914, making the case for British involvement in the war which had already started in Europe, MacDonald spoke out strongly against it, stating:

> I want to say to this House, and to say it without equivocation, if the right honourable gentleman had come here today and told us that our country is in danger, I do not care what party he appealed to, or to what class he appealed, we would be with him and behind him. If this is so, we will vote him what money he wants. Yes, and we will go farther. We will offer him ourselves if the country is in danger. But he has not persuaded me that it is. He has not persuaded my honourable friends who co-operate with me that it is, and I am perfectly certain, when his speech gets into cold print tomorrow, he will not persuade a large section of the country.[2]

MacDonald, however, found himself at odds with the pro-war majority of his own party when on 5 August 1914 the Parliamentary Labour Party voted for war credits; in doing so it disavowed its previous claims of being an internationalist workers' party and one which would never vote for war against working men in other nations. His party having made a nonsense of the anti-government line which he had put forward on its behalf only two days earlier, MacDonald promptly resigned from the chairmanship. In collaboration with a group of anti-war radicals, including Arthur Ponsonby, Charles Trevelyan, E. D. Morel and Norman Angell, he then helped to set up the Union of Democratic Control (UDC) to campaign for parliamentary control over foreign policy, negotiations with the democratic forces on the continent, and peace terms which would not humiliate the losers. By the end of the year he had become the leading figure in a bitterly unpopular but passionately committed cross-party campaign for a negotiated peace, centred on the UDC and the Independent Labour Party. Back in his constituency at Leicester, MacDonald was widely attacked for his views on the war. Although there was a strong radical element in Leicester prior to the First World War, MacDonald and his supporters in the local Labour Party were out of step with the views of most working class people in the town. There can be little doubt that, although formal politics were put aside for the duration of the war, the rift which it caused within the ranks of the local party severely compromised its position in the eyes of much of the electorate.

However MacDonald was by no means a lone voice in Leicester in 1914. Canon Frederic Donaldson, a pacifist Christian socialist minister who had been one of the leaders of the Leicester Unemployed March to London in 1905, also spoke out strongly against the war, stating:

> War betrays the innocent, crushes the weak, violates purity, destroys and devastates fair and noble cities and wrecks their habitations ... the heroism and courage evoked cannot compensate for the terrible sins of war ...[3]

MacDonald for his part moderated his views that autumn, arguing that even though his supporters opposed the war they must resign themselves to it, because they could not risk Britain being defeated; and now that the country was in the war they must see it through.

Reverend Frederic Donaldson, the radical Leicester minister who in 1914 spoke out against the war.

Private John T. Orson of the Leicestershire Yeomanry,
and his wife Mabel. They lived at 54 Ashbourne Street,
Leicester. Orson was killed in 1918.

With the outbreak of hostilities, Leicester's part-time soldiers were immediately put on a war footing. The town possessed no less than six such military units: the 3rd Battalion Leicestershire Regiment, which was a Special Reserve unit intended to train and supply recruits, and five Territorial formations. Of these latter, the 4th Battalion Leicestershire Regiment, the Leicestershire Royal Horse Artillery battery, the Leicester company of the North Midland Division Army

Service Corps and the 2nd North Midland Field Ambulance RAMC were all based at the Magazine on Oxford Street, with the Headquarters and B Squadron of the Leicestershire Yeomanry based at 48 Lincoln Street. All six units were mobilized, and the 3rd Leicesters were soon posted to the Humber defences near Hull, where they would remain throughout the war. The Territorials, however, would see front line service. They would also later be divided to form a second line (or reserve), thus the first line would be numbered 1st/4th, second line 2nd/4th, and so on.

Eliot Crawshay-Williams, until 1913 a Liberal MP for Leicester, was serving as an officer with the Leicestershire Royal Horse Artillery upon the outbreak of war. He wrote of his unit:

> We are a Battery of the Royal Horse Artillery (Territorial Force). For several years of peace we have been soldiers for a fortnight in the year. Now we have become professionals at the game - and the game has become deadly earnest. We have four

Corporal Shirley George Cartledge, 2nd/1st Battery Leicestershire Royal Horse Artillery. He lived near the Hinckley Road in Leicester.

somewhat out-of-date German-pattern guns, which are still capable of useful work (but we hope to get new English ones). Also we have a war strength, including our ammunition column, of seven officers, a doctor, a vet, nearly 250 horses, and over 200 men. In addition, of course, sundry ammunition waggons, general service waggons, water-carts, and so on, and a motley collection of stores of all kinds. That's we!

[The officers are] a mixed lot ... The men are not so mixed. They nearly all come from one large Midland town. Mostly artisans, clerks, and factory hands, with a sprinkling of the more robust trades. On the whole they may be taken to have been a difficult material for military purposes. But they had two immense advantages - wits and will. With these all things are possible. And the physique comes.[4]

Private Alfred Willis, of 63 Dorothy Road, had been serving with the 4th Leicesters since 1913 and remembered how sudden and unexpected the order to mobilize was:

Well then it was peacetime, we had three sets of uniform, two of khaki, one was the best, one was for working in, and us best scarlet ...For our annual camp in 1914 we went to Bridlington. I went with the advanced party to get all the tents and marquees up ready for the battalion coming. They were supposed to come on the Saturday, well about dinnertime they came and told us the battalion wasn't coming, because a war had broken out – that was the 4th of August ... so oh, we began to wonder ... well eventually we had to leave all that camp there ... they brought us back to Leicester, put us in some old chapel in the Friar Lane area, against the Cathedral.[5]

The eight companies of the battalion mobilized at eight different board schools across the town. Clothing and equipment were issued, and the process began of getting the battalion on to a war footing. On 12 August the battalion laid up its Colours at St Martin's church and prepared to leave Leicester. Many of its men would not see their native town again. One of the officers, Captain John Milne, has left a memorable description of the departure of the 4th Leicesters that day:

Men of the 4th Leicesters leaving the town, probably on 12 August 1914. Many of the men in this photograph would not return. (Record Office)

The Colour Party return and the battalion marches down Newarke Street; the factory windows are crowded, the streets are full. There is a group of elderly gentlemen on the steps of the Leicestershire Club; they are employers of some of the men in the ranks; they look and they wonder; they wonder what will be the end of it all.

The battalion marches on; it does not march well; the ranks are augmented by elderly men from the National Reserve, many of whom have not marched for a long time and are thoroughly out of condition. Field Service Marching Order is heavy, the day is very hot, the crowd is distracting. At the bottom of Belvoir Street it is very thick, and right up Granby Street to the Midland Station people swarm round the troops shouting farewell to their sons, sweethearts and friends; shouting to anyone and everyone, for in this time of crisis everyone speaks to his neighbour. An old, dirty-looking, motherly woman accosts a young officer as he marches in front of his company to the station. "I shall be waiting for you when you come back, me duck," she cries. He has never seen her before, and hopes he never will again, but the words stick in his memory.[6]

Following the mobilization of the Territorials, in September 1914 the Secretary of State for War, Lord Kitchener, issued an appeal for volunteers to join his New Army. Kitchener was astute enough to realize that this would be a long war, and Britain needed a mass army in order to fight it. However his distrust of the Territorial Force, based on a variety of reasons, led him to create a parallel army which would compete with it for recruits and resources, thus actually hindering British preparations for war. In 1914 Leicestershire raised four battalions in response to Kitchener's appeal: the 6th, 7th, 8th and 9th Leicesters, all designated as 'Service' battalions and comprised of men who had signed on for three years or the duration of the war, whichever was longer.

Recruits eager to sign up for the new Kitchener's Army battalions being raised in Leicester, September 1914. (Record Office)

The towering image of Kitchener (a national hero after his role in the Sudanese and Boer Wars) dominated the home of one of Leicester's most famous literary figures, the novelist C.P. Snow, who grew up in the town during the First World War. Those early months of the war were marked in Snow's memory by the endless arguments between his mother and her father-in-law, who lived with the family at 40 Richmond Road. His brother describes the household:

> Mother was deeply religious while grandfather Snow was an unbeliever, careful to keep in the single bookcase in the house the occasional theological volume which he would read diligently so as to pull the faithful to pieces with quotations from their own dogma. He was pro-Boer, more out of mischief than conviction, and after 1914 asserted that Kitchener, our mother's hero, was monumentally stupid. She in retaliation would attack her father-in-law's absolute confidence in the capacity of Belgian fortresses like Liège to keep back the Germans. He was not easily contradicted before the event since he was the only member of the family to have ventured outside England; he had been a technical adviser to several Belgian towns, including Brussels and Liège, on the installation of electric tramways. This gave him special authority when the crucial, if short-lived, extent of resistance in Belgium was in everyone's minds. He lost his fortresses and mother lost Kitchener.[7]

The outbreak of war had an immediate – if short-lived - impact on the manufacturing sector of Leicester society. The largest hosiery manufacturer in the town, Nathaniel Corah and Sons, immediately placed all of its hands on half time in anticipation (wrongly as it transpired) of a collapse in trade. Likewise Dick Read, an apprentice with Gimsons, the engineering firm, remembered:

> [I found] that the works would not be re-opening on the Monday morning, and that we were to register at the local Labour Exchange for Unemployment Insurance Benefit. Thus, in my case, the British declaration of war simply added confusion to a situation already chaotic in many respects. We had to report daily, our waiting queue gawped at by crowds of onlookers, for

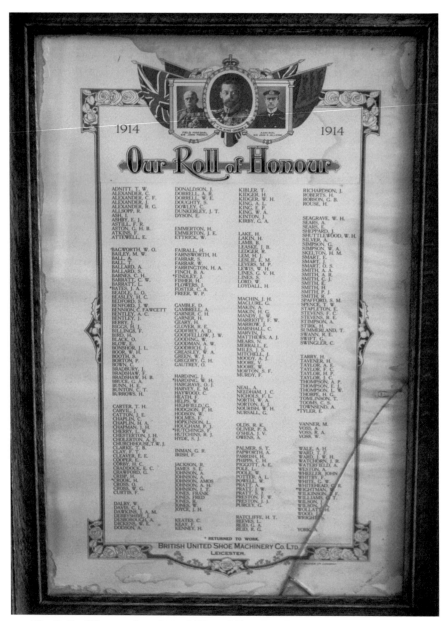

The Roll of Honour from British United Shoe Machinery in 1914, showing the names of the men from the firm who had enlisted in the army. (Courtesy of Matt Allen)

Unemployment Insurance related only to workers in engineering, ship building and coal-mining. At the end of the week we apprentices drew, I think, 6 shillings apiece benefit.

At the end of the second week we were told to report for work on the Monday morning, and for a fortnight worked hard to complete machines needed for the manufacture of army boots. Life proceeded thus until one morning we read that von Kluck – already famous – had reached the outskirts of Paris.[8]

Read and three workmates made a spur of the moment decision to enlist in the army:

[we] joined the lunchtime queue at the recruiting office in Humberstone Gate, and after a considerable wait found ourselves before two doctors and a colour sergeant. In the event, and to our great surprise, I was the only one passed as fit for service ... At this I protested, and told everyone that I wasn't going by myself. After a moment's conversation, the doctors had a look at Taylor and passed him fit. Spiers and Wade returned with us to the works, where we told our foreman that we were going and had to be sworn in at three o'clock that afternoon. He called us 'a pair of silly buggers' as he vigorously expectorated bits of chewing tobacco around the surrounding floor. Then, softening a shade, he said that if we came back, Gimsons might have a job for us. Taylor and I left hurriedly, as we had to explain matters at our digs, and we feared to be late.

We were sworn in with some pretty drunk reservists, trying to hold a corner of a tattered prayer book, drew the King's shilling and 2 shillings 9d ration allowance, and made our way to Glen Parva Barracks via the Aylestone tram.[9]

Overall, however, there was concern at the lack of response in Leicester to the appeal for volunteers for the army. The percentage of eligible men who volunteered in that autumn of 1914 was markedly lower than that in other industrial towns. The most obvious reason was not lack of patriotism, rather the fact that in Leicester there was relatively little unemployment caused by the outbreak of war. On the contrary, Leicester's chief industries, engineering, textiles and footwear, all

Reservists drawing kit at the Magazine, September 1914. (Record Office)

received large orders from the government, so there was less economic incentive to join the army, at least right away. Eric Pochin, of Goodwin Barsby engineering in Leicester, wrote later:

> The outbreak of war in August 1914, while it was the end of an era nationally and brought many changes within the life of the company, caused no break in the continuity of production. There was a brief period in the beginning of the war when doubts were expressed, but very soon the small community settled down to work out its salvation. Orders for castings, ironwork and fitments for the building trade practically ceased, and so far as the company was concerned they were never taken up again. Quarry and roadmaking machinery, however, was urgently required for the war effort, and much of this equipment was ordered by the British and allied governments. The Russian War Department placed large contracts for portable stonebreakers, with screens and bins.[10]

Likewise, in the knitwear industry it was very much business as usual, one company historian writing:

By 1913 black cardigans, pullovers and children's jerseys had built for J.Pick and sons a fine new factory at the corner of Dover and Wellington Streets … The Great War swept over it, transforming the business without seriously affecting the volume of trade. From black to khaki cardigans was not a difficult switch, and of necessity quality improved. Production was steady, contracts assured.[11]

URGENT !

Leicester Boot Manufacturers

WHO CAN MAKE

MILITARY BOOTS

And would be prepared to supply

LARGE QUANTITIES

TO A

EUROPEAN GOVERNMENT

Can see Samples and obtain Useful Information at the

"MAIL" OFFICE, 10, BELVOIR STREET,

SMALL FEE.   'Phone 1273,

Urgent pleas were made by the great and the good of Leicester to try to shore up the town's reputation in the light of what was seen as a poor response to recruiting appeals. Recruiting rallies were held in theatres and other venues, patriotic speeches were made and martial music was played. Newspapers carried advertisements and appeals for recruits for various branches of the armed forces; and indeed hundreds of men volunteered, but the perception was that Leicester's response was insufficient. Mayor Jonathan North and nine other members of the borough council wrote in an open letter to the *Leicester Mail*:

An advertisement from the Leicester press in September 1914. The outbreak of war produced unprecedented demand for the town's boot and shoe industry.

> We are well aware that many men in Leicester are working on Government contracts, and that they are doing their duty by remaining at their work of making boots, hosiery etc which are necessary for our forces; to these we make no appeal; but there are still several thousand eligible young men, sufficient to form two or three more battalions of the Leicestershire Regiment, and we feel that their country's call only needs bringing home to them, and then they will respond as others have done.[12]

Another Leicester clergyman, Reverend J.T. Coward, of St John's Church, Albion Road, told his congregation that:

> All young and eligible men ought not to be termed cowards for not forthwith joining the forces, seeing that the excessive stress

of local employment called for prompt and strenuous aid to help in adequately equipping both Navy and Army, and that was especially so in this district, hence their labours were essentially serviceable to those engaged in fighting our country's battles abroad.[13]

A Belgian refugee in Leicester, Charles Le Grand, aged 16 in January 1915, photographed in a Granby Street studio.

Coward however went on to remind his audience of the atrocities perpetrated by the Huns in their rampage through Belgium, and he, as on the whole most clergymen seem to have been, was in no doubt of the right of Britain's cause in taking up arms.

One consequence of the German drive through Belgium at the start of the war was the displacement of many thousands of Belgian civilians. Many of these people, who had left their homes with the clothes in which they stood up, and in most cases little more, had fled to England, and there was now an urgent need to distribute them around the country. A goodly number came to Leicester and the people of the town were more than willing to take them into their homes and hearts. The Belgians, after all, reminded most people of the chief reason they felt that Britain was in this war – the brutal and rapacious nature of the German army which had driven them from their homes. Sydney Gimson, the chairman of the engineering firm of that name, remembered:

> Early on [in the war], my connection with the Secular Society brought me some interesting work. I was then a member of the Town Council. When the German Army invaded Belgium and many Belgian refugees fled to England, the then Mayor, Mr Russell Frears, called a representative meeting in the Council Chamber to choose a committee who should organize the reception and care of the Belgians who were allotted to Leicester. The Committee was formed of representatives of churches, chapels, and various bodies in the town.[14]

Gimson in fact served as chairman of the Leicester Belgian Refugees

A Belgian soldier and a Leicester lady collecting money for Belgian refugees, London Road, Leicester. (Record Office)

Committee, and did much good work to assist them. Among those contributing to the support of Belgians in the town was the congregation of St Peter's Catholic Church on Leamington Street, Leicester. One of its members, a Mr J. Jarrom, made a house available for a year to accommodate at least some of them. The house, 42 Fosse Road Central, was furnished through local donations and could accommodate about thirty adults and six children. The generosity of the town in supporting Belgian refugees was not, however, without limits. Within just a few months, questions would begin to be asked in local newspapers about why young Belgian men of military age in Leicester were not enlisting in their own army, as well as concerns that some of the Belgians for who money had been pledged were more than capable of supporting themselves.

One of the consequences of the recruiting campaign on the home front was the almost immediate cessation of Rugby Football. On 2 September Mr S.C. Packer, Honorary Secretary of the Leicestershire Rugby Union, wrote:

Correspondence between Belgian refugees in Leicester and their friends and family still on the continent.

In view of the "call to arms", which is of much more importance than the active pursuit of football, the committee of the Leicestershire Rugby Union recommend that football by their affiliated clubs should be discontinued for the time being, and are of the opinion that many stalwart young men now playing should come forward and increase the strength of the British Army which is now doing doughty deeds in the fighting line.[15]

Leicester Rugby Football Club (the famous Leicester Tigers) was among the first clubs to follow this advice, and cancelled all of their fixtures for the foreseeable future on the same day as the announcement was made. The decision was greeted with appreciation by most that it was the correct and most patriotic thing to do in the circumstances.

Also in September 1914, the Aliens Restriction Act was passed, leading to the mass internment of German, and later Austro-Hungarian, citizens, many of whom had lived in Britain for many years. The move was in part at least a response to the spy hysteria that swept the country in the early months of the war. It was also to some extent for the protection of those of foreign birth, because some cities witnessed serious anti-German rioting, with the businesses of those with German-sounding names attacked and looted. In Leicester, the first Germans to be incarcerated were those who were known to be German army reservists. These men were quickly placed in military detention at Lancaster. Soon after, German civilians were also arrested. Sidney Coleman remembered:

> [There was] a very big ladies' dress shop. It was either Tylers or Taylors, the name was on the roof in big gilded letters. About 1910 it closed down, and a German came and made it into a beautiful delicatessen store, which the Leicester people had never seen, and they haven't seen one [like it] since. And he wasn't naturalized, and so when the First World War started he was interned, and the shop was closed and boarded up.[16]

Lieutenant Kenneth Berridge Wood, Machine Gun Corps. The son of a hosiery manufacturer from Leicester, Wood played for Leicester Tigers and represented Great Britain in the 1910 Rugby Union tour of South Africa.

Perhaps the most prominent German family in Leicester were the Wildt brothers. Hans and Herman Wildt were the owners of Wildt & Co Hosiery Machine Builders, of Adelaide Works in The Newarkes. Upon the outbreak of war, anti-German feeling was such that in October 1914 the youngest member of the family, Edwin 'Teddy' Wildt, appears to have fled to the United States, where he continued to develop and patent textile machinery.

Anti-German feeling however was not universal in Leicester. One religious, thoughtful and intelligent young man, Albert Parr, a clerk in an engineering factory, had before the war been heavily influenced by socialism and indeed by the writings of Karl Marx, which caused him to question the inequalities which he had seen in England prior to the war. Parr, writing shortly after the outbreak of the conflict, stated:

> I wonder, many times, what those three great beloved, and world-renowned Germans, Johann Christoph Friedrich von Schiller, Heinrich Heine, and Wilhelm Richard Wagner, would have said and written about the terrible crimes and unnameable

outrages that have been perpetrated by their fellow countrymen in innocent and peaceful little Belgium, were they alive today.[17]

Nonetheless, he had this to say about those living Germans closer at hand:

My German friend in Leicester is a bit of a philosopher, for he says that no nation, however prosperous and powerful she may be, can exist without the support and patronage of another. And the sooner the nations of the earth realise this, and the one common brotherhood of man, so much the better. He even goes farther, and says that no man, whatever nation he may belong to, can live, and enjoy the many comforts of life, without the industry and support of another. He is an interesting and quiet spoken man, a lover of art and peace, and I have come to love and respect him. There certainly is an abounding truth in the words of my German friend.[18]

Albert Parr, the young Leicester man whose loyalty to his German friend outweighed national sentiment.

We cannot be certain, but it seems probable that, in spite of his love of peace, if Parr's German friend was of military age he would have spent most of the next four years behind barbed wire in a prisoner of war camp on the Isle of Man. Another young Leicester man devoid of anti-German prejudice was Sydney Pick, manager of the family knitwear firm. The company historian tells us:

The man whose help he valued most during those rough years was Theodore Trost. Representative of a great wholesaler, Trost was of German origin and 1914-18 were not the best years for Germans in British business. He grew used to hostility, but that did not make him like it better or suffer less. S.J. Pick was one of the few men who didn't care whether Trost was born in Munich or Bootle: he liked and admired him, and that was enough. Trost in turn warmed to this young man struggling in a stormy sea. Their first contact was a lesson Sydney never forgot.

Trost ordered officers' cardigans. Sydney, brought up in a cheeseparing tradition and wanting to impress with a neat stroke of business, cut the price. Trost took one look and said: "This is not what I asked for."

"Er – well, it's just as good, and it will save you a lot of money."

Trost swung a heavy arm. "Look here, young man, let's understand one another from the start; if I had wanted to spend less money I would have ordered another garment. I ordered exactly what I wanted and was prepared to pay for it, and I have not got it. What is to be done about that?"

No more cheeseparing, Sydney determined; and there was no more.[19]

Sometimes the difficulty lay in establishing who was a German, and who was not. A clicker in a shoe factory from Preston Street, a man named Mark Isenstein, found himself in the Borough Police Court charged with being an enemy alien and not registering under the 1914 Act. The defendant protested that he was a Russian Jew, even though he had never worshipped with other Jews in Leicester and was married to an English woman. Asked by the court if he could prove his nationality, Isenstein stated:

All I know is that my father was a Russian, but he has been dead six years.[20]

In spite of the fact that a borough councillor was prepared to vouch for him and gave a statement that the man was a valuable member of society who was well liked at his place of work, the court was taking no chances and bound Isenstein over in the sum of £5 to appear again if summonsed. It seems that someone at the time must have had an idea that all was not as it was claimed to be, for now we can see that both the 1901 and 1911 censuses record Isenstein as actually born in Germany.

Meanwhile, on the battlefields of the Western Front, Leicester soldiers were involved in the battles of the Aisne and La Bassée, and the first reports began to filter back of men from the town who had been killed or wounded. Newspapers were filled with portrait photos

A rare photo of Leicester Church Lads Brigade Cadet Corps, about to lead a parade through the town on 10 October 1914. Note the obsolete Martini Henry rifles.

of men in smart red pre-war uniforms, or in some cases starched white tunics, taken whilst the men were stationed on the hot dusty plains of India. In most cases the men had been killed, and the newspapers carried short snippets of information about each one: 'he had spent seven years on the corporation tramways'; or 'he leaves a widow at Ranikhet in India'.

We have a particular insight into the experiences of one Leicester soldier in these battles. Private George Dodge kept a diary of events, leading up to and including the action in which he was taken prisoner by the Germans, which was part of the Battle of Armentières-La Bassée in October 1914. Dodge and his comrades in the 1st Battalion Leicestershire Regiment were tasked with defending a railway line against an almost overwhelming German attack. It was at the level crossing south of La Houssoie that Dodge's D Company came under severe pressure. He wrote:

[The] Company ... must hold out at all costs, at night [24 October] all ammunition spent and surrounded by enemy. By dawn [25 October] back to back fighting with 85 men using dead as cover. Hand to hand fighting, finally at 10am made prisoners by at least an Army Corps sweeping down on us. Night march to German headquarters, humiliated and searched. Prisoners put in a cell at Lille prison and given black bread and water.[21]

Among the Leicesters fighting here was a former forward with Leicester Rugby Football Club named William Dalby. An army reservist, Dalby had been recalled to the Colours upon the outbreak of war. In a letter home, he described the attack:

> The sentries in the trenches … shout "Stand To, everybody," and this wakens our men … then the Maxim guns send between 600 and 700 shots per minute, the Field Artillery fire shrapnel rockets, and search lights illuminate the sky for miles around, 'star shells' set fire to haystacks, the Garrison artillery set fire to the villages and knock down anything else that comes in the way. The whizzing and whirring of shot and shell sounds as if every man had gone whistling mad. You cannot hear yourself shout.

Private George Dodge, 1st Battalion Leicestershire Regiment. Dodge was captured by the Germans near Rue du Bois on 25 October 1914. His parents lived at 17 Flint Street, in the Highfields area of Leicester.

It is like this for an hour or two, then the German big guns stop firing. That is the signal for their infantry to charge. They come up in thousands singing 'Wacht am Rhein' and blowing penny trumpets and making as much noise as possible. They get within a few yards of our trenches and find our fire too hot for them.[22]

Some of those wounded in the early actions of the war would be treated at the 5th Northern General Hospital in Leicester. Some of the buildings on this site now form part of the University of Leicester, but in 1914 this was the County Lunatic Asylum. In common with other similar facilities in Britain, it had been designated before the war as a Territorial Force hospital, and once hostilities began it was adapted to treat military casualties. One of the earliest patients was Quartermaster Sergeant Williams of the 2nd Battalion Suffolk Regiment. He had shown great bravery at the Battle of the Marne in September 1914, where he was badly wounded, having part of his leg shot away. Williams had acquired a trophy in the form of a German artillery

Sergeant Williams of the Suffolk Regiment shows off a trophy of war to two nurses at the 5th Northern General Hospital, Leicester, in 1914.

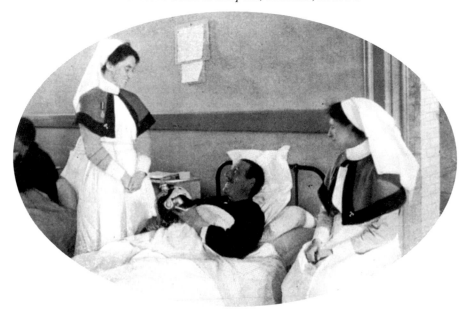

officer's spiked pickelhaube helmet, which he had carried strapped to his haversack for four days before being wounded. Even the trauma of losing his leg on the battlefield could not induce Williams to be parted from his trophy, and he was pictured showing it off to nurses who were treating him at hospital in Leicester in October 1914.

However, it was not just military casualties who were treated there. As a very young child, Mrs A. Overton was injured in the German naval bombardment of Hartlepool in December 1914. Her house received a direct hit and she was buried among the debris. As soon as she could be moved she was sent to Leicester for treatment. She remembered that,

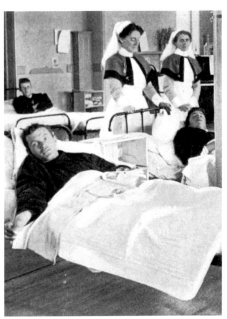

A scene inside the 5th Northern General Hospital, early in the war.

When I was able to travel, swathed in bandages with head injuries and two splinters of shrapnel still in my left leg, we were evacuated to Leicester because Mother's father lived here, in Burley's Lane. He was steward of the Manchester WMC on Humberstone Gate. He had got Mam a house in Bedford Street, near a herbalist's shop.[23]

She then became a patient at the hospital and remembered:

I still clearly remember Sister Aldwinckle (I thought her name was Old Winkle for years). She was very good to me and on my third birthday she made me a little red jelly and a small sponge cake for my tea. The 'Tommies' in the ward bought me a lovely 'rag' picture book of the New Testament stories, via a nurse. ... The family moved to another house, 134 Crafton Street. When I left hospital I went there, still heavily bandaged, partly disabled and now an out-patient at the Base Hospital.[24]

Despite its landlocked status, and its claim to be the town farthest from the sea, Leicester's men were serving in good numbers in the Royal Navy as well as in the army. One of the earliest to see active service afloat was J. Whyley, of HMS *Carnarvon*, who took part in the Battle of the Falkland Islands in December 1914. He wrote to his parents in Merridale Road, Humberstone:

> We have been in action, and have sunk five German men-of-war. We were fighting for about five and a half hours, and steaming at full speed all the time. We started to chase them about half past four in the morning, and the first shot was fired at five minutes to one. The first German ship sank about twenty minutes past four in the afternoon, the second about six o'clock, and we had sunk all the five by nine o'clock. And the best of it was we never had a casualty on our ship, and altogether our ships only lost seven killed and about 40 wounded. So you see it was a glorious victory. It has given Germany a big kick in the neck. The worst of it was that while we were picking up what survivors we could we saw bodies with no heads and some cut in two floating by…[25]

A group of Sea Scouts in Leicester. Despite its distance from the coast, Leicester would send considerable numbers of men to the Royal Navy during the Great War.

At Christmas, the *Leicester Daily Mercury* organized parcels for the men of the Leicestershire Regiment at the front. The men deeply appreciated these gifts, and in consequence their thoughts turned to home. Lance Corporal Thompson, writing to the newspaper to express his thanks, stated:

> At the time of writing the boys are all having breakfast and the topic is Leicester, and the praise of the directors of the 'Post' and 'Mercury' is simple and genuine. Pte Tom Pagan, who lives not a mile from the Clock Tower, has already 'waffled' his chocolate, his excuse being, "Its so nice, somebody might want mine as well". He is now ensconced in a corner, writing pad on his knee, writing home for more of Cadbury's 'Mexican'.[26]

Telegraphist George Fisher RNVR of Leicester, who served in the Royal Navy on minesweeping duties as part of the Dover Patrol. After the war he taught at the City Boys School for thirty years.
(Courtesy of Ann Jessop)

The *Mercury* was not alone in sending out supplies to local soldiers that Christmas; an Old Boy of Bridge Road School, Driver Hainsworth of the Royal Horse Artillery, wrote back to his former headmaster:

> I have received the presents from the school. I was very pleased with them. It is very good of the school children, and I am sure the Bridge Road Old Boys much appreciate the spirit in thinking of the old boys at the front…[27]

Leicester soldiers in France participated in the famous 1914 Christmas Truce, looking out over cold snowy fields near Bois Grenier. In spite of the ceasefire, which had held for most of the morning and afternoon, one man was actually sniped on Christmas Day. Lance Corporal George Sutton of Leicester was shot and killed late on the afternoon of 25 December. His

Fisher's identity disc, showing that Leicester naval reservists were enrolled in the Bristol Port Division. (Courtesy of Ann Jessop)

friend, Private Bernard Smith, who in civilian life had lived a few streets away, was standing next to him at the time and the memory of the tragic incident remained with him for the remainder of his days. At Christmas back home in Leicester in later years, he would recount to his daughter the story of how a German shouted a warning, but a shot followed all too quickly and Sutton was unable to reach cover.

Two Leicester comrades: Lance Corporal George Sutton (standing) was killed on Christmas Day 1914 in the trenches near Rue du Bois; his friend, Private Bernard Smith (seated), was nearby when it happened.

CHAPTER 2

War most cruel

Even though it was not yet six months old, the war was throwing social and human relationships into sharper focus than ever before. As it progressed, it would blow away the stuffy conventions and formal behaviour of Victorian Britain, as young men and young women realized that their moments of happiness together were fleeting. Often liaisons were given added poignancy by the thought that a young man might soon be leaving for France, with the very real possibility that he might not return. Leicester was the scene for one such romantic tryst

The station of the Midland Railway in Leicester, scene of the romantic liaison between Vera Brittain and Roland Leighton.

Midland Station, Leicester

in January 1915. Vera Brittain, a promising student at Oxford, had before Christmas been introduced to a young army officer named Roland Leighton. Though their meetings had been closely chaperoned to ensure respectability, the two had quickly fallen in love and contrived now to meet out of sight and earshot of maiden aunts. By taking a different train from her home at Buxton back to Oxford, Vera could spend a few precious hours alone with Roland, who had found an excuse to be away from his unit. Vera remembered:

> At Leicester, Roland, who had started from Peterborough soon after dawn, was waiting for me with another sheaf of pale pink roses. He looked tired, and said he had a cold; actually, it was incipient influenza and he ought to have been in bed, but I did not discover this till afterwards.
>
> To be alone with one another after so much observation was quite overwhelming, and for a time conversation in the Grand Hotel lounge moved somewhat spasmodically. But constraint disappeared when he told me with obvious pride that he had asked his own colonel for permission to interview the colonel of the 5th Norfolks, who were stationed some distance away and were shortly going to the front, with a view to getting a transfer.
>
> "Next time I see the C.O.," he announced, "I shall tell him the colonel of the 5th was away. I shall say I spent the whole day looking for him – so after lunch I'm coming with you to Oxford."
>
> I tried to subdue my leaping joy by a protest about his cold, but as we both knew this to be insincere it was quite ineffective. I only stipulated that when we arrived he must lose me at the station.[1]

Their romantic tryst in the lavish surroundings of one of Leicester's most prestigious hotels must have been a world away from the day-to-day reality of life for most ordinary people in the town. Whilst some industries in Leicester prospered as a result of the war, notably clothing, boots and engineering (all of which had military purpose) other trades were suffering severely due to the disruption in normal commercial life. Frank Ashmore, of the Leicester branch of the National Society of Operative House and Ship Painters, stated that:

It is estimated that there are at the present time as many as 50 per cent of the Leicester Operative Painters out of employment, a percentage, it need hardly be said, far in excess of the normal for the time of year. Much distress exists among this class in consequence, and unless work is soon forthcoming this distress must grow rapidly.[2]

Other independent small businessmen suffered equal hardship as the downturn in trade affected their livelihoods. Charles Bacon, a carrier and removal man from Belgrave Gate, had before the war built his business up from being a single man with a horse drawn dray to owner of a motor lorry employing several men. Just prior to the outbreak of war, business was so good that he had taken out a lease purchase upon a parcel of land, in order to build a garage for his van. The outbreak of hostilities took away most of his workmen and much of his trade. Bacon remembered wistfully:

A few weeks after that we lost more men, but I would like to recall a few of the happy hours and the many talks I had with several of the men who worked along with me during those years. I know most of their bodies lie in France but their spirits and companionship still live … I have often thought that time like an ever rolling stream bears all its sons away. Some of them have died and some had to leave me for the war, most of them are departed, all are gone now, those old familiar faces.[3]

Despite the hardship of being in a position in which they had to meet fixed payments, even though there was a downturn in business, he and his wife struggled on. On one occasion they managed to avoid defaulting on their payments only because Mrs Bacon's father was able to give them some money from his savings to keep them afloat. Bacon also records the fact that during the war he stored furniture for those men who were away fighting. Because working men tended to rent property rather than own it, they may well have sent wives and children to live with parents whilst they were away in the army.

Perhaps surprisingly, Bacon makes no mention in his extensive memoirs of the requisition by the army of any of his horses. Though this undoubtedly did occur in many places at the start of the war, and

A typical Leicester hosiery factory, on Curzon Street.

indeed Leicester Cattle Market became a marshalling centre for the assembly of horses collected from the countryside, by 1915 the army had moved away from compulsory purchase of these animals and instead used the open market to acquire its remounts. Nevertheless, the loss of dray horses from the towns, as well as agricultural horses from the fields, did much to accelerate the switch from horse power to the internal combustion engine both during the war and afterwards.

In the Leicester hosiery trade the greatest threat came from the fact that more than ninety per cent of the needles used in the industry came from Germany, the Germans having cornered the market in production of these vital pieces of equipment. In spite of the demand from the army for clothing, in January 1915 in Leicester there was hosiery machinery standing idle due to the shortage of needles and urgent steps were being taken to source new supplies within Britain.

Whilst some called for government intervention in this matter, there were already creeping signs of increasing official interference in daily life, and it was not welcome. Before the war's end, the government would control almost every aspect of the life of the citizen, ranging from what he could eat to whether he should be in the army or not, something unthinkable just a few years earlier. The first signs of this came with the order to close licensed premises by 9pm, ostensibly to keep newly enlisted young soldiers away from the temptation of alcohol. In January 1915, No 1 Branch of the National Union of Boot and Shoe Operatives met in Leicester and resolved that:

> This meeting, representing 9000 members ... protests against the action of the military authorities in closing licensed houses at so early an hour as 9pm, on the grounds that it is an uncalled for interference with the liberty of the subject, that it is unnecessary ... and that it inflicts a hardship on many of the members of our trade who are working overtime in order to cope with Government orders.[4]

Yet even for those in full employment, by early 1915 the effects of the war on daily life on the home front were beginning to make themselves felt. In Leicester it was estimated that the wholesale prices of foodstuffs had risen by between fifteen and twenty per cent. This however masked the fact that sugar had risen in price a hundred per cent as a result of extra duty; tea also had risen in price through extra duty. Many cereals had risen by fifty per cent. The only staple that had not risen dramatically was home-produced bacon, the price of which had remained stable simply because more farmers had been forced to kill

Soldiers of the 4th Leicesters marching along Oxford Street. Their kit is piled on a wagon in the livery of the Great Central Railway, indicating their destination. The fact that they are wearing greatcoats suggests this is a reinforcement draft, early in 1915. (Record Office)

their pigs through shortages of feed. Bread prices had also increased on four occasions since the outbreak of war; most wheat was imported from the United States. To cap it all, coal, which every household depended upon, had also risen in price to £2 per ton, four shillings more per ton than the price before Christmas. This was a consequence both of a fall in production due to the numbers of miners who had joined the army and difficulty in obtaining supplies because of government demands on the railways.

Recruits continued to volunteer, though as in 1914 the numbers were still disappointing. Denis Dougherty worked in Leicester as a carpenter with the building firm of Bentleys. He had wanted to enlist in the army in 1914, though he was not prepared to lie about his age in order to do so:

> I wanted to join, but two things prevented me – my apprenticeship and the fact that I was under age, though I might have got in as many did by stating they were eighteen. The firm had lost two joiners with the Territorials and a yard labourer as a Reservist, and put up a notice stating that apprentices would be allowed to break their indentures at the age of eighteen years if they desired to join the forces, but it would be incumbent on them to serve another year on the conclusion of the war. Alex Stevenson, our senior, was of age, and had permission to join up; [he joined] the carpenters' crew of the Royal Navy.[5]

Dougherty was impressed by the sight of a party of newly recruited Territorials singing as they marched through Stoneygate, where he was working on a house on London Road. Following his birthday in February 1915 he resolved to enlist, also hoping to join the carpenters' crew:

> I obtained permission to break my apprenticeship and went to the Royal Navy Recruiting Office in Southgate Street. I was passed medically fit, except for a slight fault in my right eye. The Marine Sergeant forwarded my application and said he would keep me informed when my papers came through. So I returned to work to await the outcome.[6]

In the event, Dougherty was not accepted into the navy as a carpenter, but was offered the position of stoker, which he declined. He resolved instead to join the army. His was a similar story to that of Jack Horner, a working class lad who had been born in a 'one up, one down' house in Court D, Wellington Street, Leicester, which was rented by his parents for half a crown a week. Horner remembered many years later that the long hours and poor wages in industry at this time were as much of an incentive for joining the army as was patriotism:

> It was a cold grey day on 12 March 1915, when my pal, Bill Hill and I, were going back to work in the afternoon. I was in the engineering trade, Billy in the shoe industry. I was working 48 hours per week for a wage of seven shillings per week and one and a half pence a day for going in at 7 o'clock in the morning to light the fires

Private Jack Horner, 8th Leicesters, wearing an ill-fitting suit of khaki, around the time of his enlistment in March 1915.

> – that was my spending money, spent in riotous living – a piece of fish with chips, on a plate, and eaten in a fish and chip shop in Church Gate, all for two pence, then later, seated in the Gods at the Palace … the doors opened, and there was a race for the front seats, to see all the great stars of variety, all for two pence. I was just over 17 years old at that time and, on the way to work, we were discussing things in general, when one of us, I don't recall who, suggested that we go and join the army. No sooner said than done! We made our way to the Recruiting Office … [and] saw the Sergeant who told us he was very busy as some reservists had been called to the Colours. He gave us two pence each to get a tram to Saffron Lane, and [then] walk to Wigston Barracks.[7]

Horner and Bill Hill notwithstanding, there had still been proportionately fewer men enlisting in Leicester than from other comparable towns, and Councillor Mr Hincks moved a motion on 30 March 1915:

That this council deplores the scanty response of Leicester men to the recruiting appeals.[8]

The statistics that Hincks produced spoke for themselves. In Newcastle and Nottingham, 18.5% of the male population had joined the Colours. In Swansea it was 10.5%, Wakefield 7.6%, Hull 7.1%, Manchester and Sheffield both 6.7%, Leeds 5.5%, Derby 5.2%, Bradford 4.1%, Oldham 4.0% and finally Leicester at 2.6%. Interestingly, four out of the lowest five were predominantly textile towns, and these statistics may reflect relatively higher employment (and wages) in these places due to Government contracts. Another major hindrance to recruiting in Leicester was undoubtedly the poor physical state of numerous young working-class men. Having left school in adolescence, perhaps already undernourished, many of these men had gone straight into long and arduous labour in factories, which had further restricted their physical development. Colonel Charles Yate, MP for the Melton division, observed that:

… in Leicester, we have the known percentage of 27½ rejected as unfit, in addition, remember, to those men who knew that they could not come up to the standard and never presented themselves for enlistment at all. What that number in the country is, of course, we cannot guess, but we all believe it to be very large. I know that in the General Annual Report of the British Army for 1912, it is stated that in the six years, from 1906 to 1911, nearly 40 per cent of the men who offered themselves were rejected on physical grounds before attestation, and that in addition 3½ per cent were rejected after attestation. Remember, the standard required was much higher then than the standard required now. It just shows how few men were able to come up to it.

It is not only in the standard of height that our men fail at the present time, but also in the standard of chest measurement. Five feet one inch, or five feet three inches is not the proper standard of height of the British race. The fact that the War Office, have been obliged to lower the standard for recruits to five feet one inch of itself shows how our national physique is deteriorating.[9]

Recruiting staff at Leicester Town Hall in 1915. On the right stands Colour Sergeant Yeomans. (Record Office)

Efforts to encourage more men to volunteer came from numerous directions. In the music halls, many *artistes* used their position to call upon men to enlist. One, the Scottish comedian Harry Lauder, went even further and assembled his own pipe band with which he toured the country, encouraging recruits. The band visited Leicester in the early months of 1915 and Lauder remembered:

> It was as great a surprise tae me as it could ha' been to anyone else when I discovered that I could move men and women by speakin' tae them. In the beginning, in Britain, I made speeches to help the recruiting. My boy John had gone frae the first, and through him I knew much about the army life, and the way of it in those days. Sae I began to mak' a bit speech, sometimes, after the show. And then I organized my recruiting band— Hieland laddies, wha went up and doon the land, skirling the pipes and beating the drum. The laddies wad flock to hear them, and when they were brocht together so there was easy work for the sergeants who were wi' the band. There's something about the skirling of the pipes that fires a man's blood and sets his feet and his fingers and a' his body to tingling.[10]

That spring, a variety of semi-autonomous home-grown units proliferated across the borough. The Leicester Junior Training Corps, an organization which had been formed before Christmas the previous year, aimed to prepare youngsters who were as yet too young for military service. It soon attracted approving comments, Colonel Yate once again remarked:

A lapel badge of the Leicester Junior Training Corps.

I had the honour the other day of inspecting the Leicester Junior Training Corps at drill in a large skating rink [probably the Granby Halls]. There I found some 2,000 odd boys, of ages ranging from 16 to 19, all voluntarily drilling away and doing their best to develop their bodies by learning the drill that ought to have been taught to them at school. Here were these boys spending their time at drill at night, after working hours, and trying their best, voluntarily, to make up for the deficiency in their education. All credit to these boys, I say; and all credit to the generous people who have helped them and enabled them to obtain that drill of which they were so much in need. I mention this to show what a demand there is in the country for cadet training, and how much cadet training would add to the popularity, both of our county council schools and of our continuation schools.[11]

The Leicester Motor Corps, which had been re-established the previous August in response to the outbreak of war, consisted of owners of private cars, motorcycles and sidecar combinations, who agreed to act as a form of mobile home defence force. By the spring of 1915 they were well organized. At Easter of that year the Commandant, C.F. Bray, organized an exercise in which the drivers assembled with their machines at the Magazine Square, before motoring to the east coast to take part in training with other mobile forces. By this stage in the war the Corps came under the auspices of the Leicestershire Territorial Association, and the drivers had been equipped with khaki uniforms and rifles. They were not the only volunteers in the borough. Leicester's Volunteer Training Corps, the First World War equivalent of the Home Guard, practised drilling and marching in the Borough

A member of the Leicester Motor Corps, with his Rudge motorcycle and sidecar combination, outside the Great Northern Railway station on Belgrave Road.

parks and by this point in the war, and taking these volunteer units together, they numbered some 3000 men.

The government however remained suspicious of the Volunteers for most of the war; at best it felt that they were a distraction, at worst they threatened to compete for resources and manpower with the new armies now being raised; indeed there was more than a whiff of official suspicion that they were harbouring men who ought to have enlisted for active service. The government did nothing to support them and provided no weapons or clothing; in fact during 1915 questions were actually raised about the legality of such corps bearing arms. The members wore civilian clothing with a brassard bearing the letters 'G.R'. Although it stood for 'Georgius Rex', this was popularly misquoted as 'Gorgeous Wrecks', whilst other wags claimed that it stood for 'Genuine Relics' or 'Grandpa's Regiment'. It was not surprising that with official hostility and with no arms or uniforms forthcoming, initial enthusiasm for the Volunteers began to melt away; many of the older men drifted into the open and welcoming arms of the Leicester Special Constabulary, which was also undergoing expansion.

Around this time, March 1915, news began to filter through to Leicester of the Battle of Neuve Chapelle, the first real British success on the Western Front since it had settled into trench warfare, and more particularly of the part played in it by the 2nd Battalion Leicestershire Regiment. Using a rapid bombardment and surprise as a tactic, British and Indian troops had managed to wrest back the German-held village. Though the enemy had rapidly recovered from being caught off-guard, and nothing like a break-through was achieved, the battle boosted morale in the BEF. The news of the victory was particularly significant for Leicester people, for it soon became known that one of their own, Leicester-born William Buckingham, had been awarded the Victoria Cross for his exploits in the battle. There was a good deal of excitement as this was Leicester's first VC of the war. Buckingham

Private Arthur Beaumont, 2nd Battalion Leicestershire Regiment. He grew up at 5 Northgate Street, Leicester, and took part in the battalion's early actions on the Western Front.

returned home wounded and was interviewed by the local press. Clearly a shy and unassuming man, it was difficult for journalists at first to glean anything of his experiences, but gradually his story emerged:

> During the battle I came upon a badly wounded German soldier. One of his legs had been blown off. He was lying right in the fire zone. His piteous appeal for help – well, I rendered him first aid as well as I could, and just carried him to a place of safety! I did what I could, of course, for others too – but there, it's really not worth talking about![12]

Showing the scars from a gunshot wound to the chest, he continued:

> It was a near thing. It would have been all over but for a packet of postcards in my left breast pocket. The bullet passed through the cards and entered my chest on the left side. It was, however, deflected and came out on the right side, when it was again deflected by my cartridge case and lodged in my right arm, just above the elbow. There I carried it till I got to the South Manchester Hospital.[13]

Away from the Western Front, in the Dardanelles, a bold plan championed by Winston Churchill was underway, with the objectives both of knocking Turkey out of the war and of getting supplies to Russia in order to keep her in it. However, the Royal Navy had conspicuously failed to force its way through the Narrows into the Black Sea. A combination of Turkish shore batteries and minefields had accounted for a number of British and French warships and, belatedly, on 25 April, the army was thrown in to attempt to capture the Turkish positions guarding the straits and neutralize them. With any element of surprise lost, it was to be an ill-fated campaign. An eyewitness to these events was a Leicester sailor, George Draper, a Leading Stoker in HMS *Implacable*. Draper had joined the navy in 1908, so he was an old hand. He recalled many years later:

> When we left Lemnos we took aboard 500 Lancashire Fusiliers and 250 of the Royal Fusiliers as well and a certain number of naval brigade people ... we steamed in and the *River Clyde* steamed alongside... and they ran her aground so the lads could go down these brows onto the beach. We of course had to land ours, with a picket boat towing cutters ... and land ours that way. We were very lucky, we got all ours ashore without a single casualty to the troops ... the *River Clyde*, the boat that was alongside of us, she was very unfortunate. Where they ran ashore, the troops had to jump off the bows into the water, the Turks had put a belt of barbed wire under the water ... they were sitting ducks ...a big percentage were killed, others were wounded and taken away by the *Implacable*'s boats to hospital ships that lay further out... [I could see this happening because] we were within three hundred yards of the shore, we were a battleship, the upper deck guns were four 12 pounders each side, and of course there was the 6 inch guns in the turrets, and we had 12 inch guns ... two forrard and two aft...[14]

Back in Leicester, as across much of Britain, a new trade union was now gathering strength. Previously in the town, only craftsmen, and the boot and shoe and hosiery workers were unionized. In the engineering trade, only the very skilled were organized; the semi-skilled and labourers had no voice at all. However, unlike most other unions, which were narrowly based upon a trade or craft, the Workers' Union appealed to the mass of unskilled or semi-skilled workers (many of them women) who had previously been unrepresented by the existing unions, and who were now flooding into industry. Prominent in this organization was Sydney Taylor, who in 1913 had walked to Leicester from Coventry, a distance of twenty-four miles, in search of work. He soon found a job as a carpenter, working on shop fronts; Taylor had previous experience in the Amalgamated Society of Carpenters and Joiners and, as an enthusiastic trade unionist and a socialist, he began to try to organize a Leicester branch of the Workers' Union. Initially he had just thirteen members, but the conditions produced by the war encouraged rapid expansion. Taylor recalled later:

Sydney Taylor, leader of the Leicester branch of the Workers' Union during the First World War. (Courtesy of Ned Newitt)

> In April 1915 I was invited by Mr J. Beard, the National President of the Workers' Union, to take on a job as District Organiser at the large wage of 35/- per week. After giving it thought with my wife I accepted and in six months I got 1000 new members and a 5/- per week rise.[15]

Much of Taylor's work focused upon the engineering industry, and his first real fight was with the engineering employers. Eventually a twenty three shilling minimum wage for unskilled labourers was agreed, with an additional four shillings for some semi-skilled men in engineering works and foundries. He also fought for and won overtime pay for foundry labourers. In the early part of the war there was a great deal of dilution in the engineering workforce, as fit men joined the army and semi-skilled men or women were put on to machines in their place. Taylor insisted on the dilutees receiving the full rate for the work that they were doing. This brought them into conflict with established engineering unions, who complained that the contributions required by the Workers' Union were lower than their own and who insisted the newcomers should have joined them. Ironically, in these early days the majority of members joined the Workers' Union because no other union was interested in them. On the whole these men and women were not interested in political struggles; their main concern was in improving their wages.

For Taylor, like his members, the overriding priority was improving pay and wherever possible he tried to work in co-operation with employers to achieve this. He believed that by keeping his finger on the pulse of his membership he could generally nip grievances in the bud, and he advised against strikes unless absolutely necessary. As an example of the close relationship that Taylor enjoyed with some employers, during the First World War he was the first trade union official to enter the offices of W.A. Bates & Co, elastic web manufacturers, at St Mary's Mills, on the southern edge of Leicester. At that time the highest wage paid was twenty eight shillings for a fifty-four hour week in the motorcycle tyre shop. Taylor asked the managing director for an increase in wages for the workforce, but was told that the firm could not afford it. Taylor then advised the managing director to go over to piecework, which he agreed to try. Soon afterwards the managing director complained that wage costs had now doubled; Taylor told him that he should be delighted, because production had also doubled, whilst overheads remained the same. Consequently piecework remained, at the same rate. So good did relations between Taylor and the firm become that they supplied him with free tyres for his bicycle, which he used to reach union branches in outlying towns, sometimes covering fifty miles a day. When, later in the war, the union provided him with a motorcycle and sidecar for this work, Bates also supplied him with free tyres for this as well. After 1916, Taylor would become the only trade union official of military age in Leicester, so important was his work that he was exempted from military service.

There was less harmony between management and unions at the dye works in Leicester where Tom Barclay was employed during the war; possibly the best men were away at the front and the management were struggling to find suitable workers, though Barclay makes no mention of any female labour:

Tom Barclay, socialist and secularist, who was employed at a Leicester dye works during the First World War.

I have worked at quite twenty factories in Leicester during the last fifty years, but the lot of men who worked there were the worst I ever sampled. There was a hustling, bustling chap, said to be an "American," a specialist worker in something; there were three or four men, since dead, on the verge of imbecility but not lacking muscle; their shoulders stooped, their mouths hung, and they shambled in their walk, but they had muscle: there was a malignant humbug who watched and dodged the managers and shirked all he could, and a patient honest rather old man victimized into doing more than his share through the shirking of the malignant; a sycophantic crawler ready to put up with anything, and a man who, it was said, had been a manager and seemed anxious to be one again. These are a few specimens of from seventy to eighty hands who sneered at one another, barged one another, and worked against instead of in harmony with one another. Managers sauntered and prowled, but seemed unable to distinguish between the humbugging shirkers and the straightforward hands who were doing their best. Now and then, one of the "heads" moved about, silent, rigid, smileless, aloof; no vizier or czar could be more distant and important looking.[16]

The dye industry in Leicester took on renewed prominence during the First World War, mainly supplying the Admiralty, which before the war had obtained nearly all its supplies from the dominant German dye industry (which, deprived of its overseas markets, had largely turned its attention to making chemical weapons). Tom Barclay had been born in poverty in Leicester's slums. Mainly self-educated, he was a committed socialist and secularist, having disavowed the Roman Catholicism of his Irish immigrant roots. In his younger days he had been a leader of the hosiery workers' union in Leicester, and he attributes the discord among the workers in the dye works at which he found himself during the Great War to the fact that there was so little union representation. Barclay continues:

At the aforesaid Works I was but a casual hand, a dyer's labourer, an old man. Well the dyers who were Trade Unionists, obtained an advance in wages, and that made some of the rest of us discontented. We began to agitate, and the heads of the firm came to hear of it and summoned one of the ring-leaders.

"You've been trying to get the men to join the Union" said a 'head'.

"Yes," said the ring-leader, "I believe in a living wage, and we're not getting it."

"Do you know what we do with hands that agitate like that?"

"You can do what you like, Sir; if you sack me I can get another place, and my Trade Union'll defend me till I do."[17]

In the event, the troublesome hand was not sacked, suggesting that either labour was in such short supply that the firm could not afford to lose the man, or that they feared the backlash from his union. Barclay, for his part, lamented the fact that the working class of Leicester did not show sufficient solidarity to lift themselves from wage slavery. He felt that for every one who was active in a union, others around him were either too interested in football or horse racing to support him, or too beguiled by religion and focused solely upon salvation in the next world.

As might be expected from one of his strong political beliefs, the war seems to have found little support with Barclay. He was a life-long admirer of George Bernard Shaw, the Irish playwright and philosopher, who vehemently opposed British involvement in the conflict. When Shaw was savaged in the press in 1914 for publishing his essay *Common Sense about the War*, Barclay wrote to him:

I can't remain silent in face of your letter to the *Daily Chronicle*. Unfortunately my support of you cannot have public utterance as I am a nonentity; still I feel I must write to you ...[18]

Barclay concluded his letter by expressing his disappointment that other socialists had not rallied to the call of Shaw, who he regarded as the deepest and wisest thinker of his age. In spite of what Barclay believed, the Leicester branch of the Independent Labour Party did remain resolute in its anti-war stance. The branch newsletter *Monthly Notes* from this period stated:

The attitude of the ILP towards the War, its loyalty to its former peace ideals, and its invincible faith in Internationalism have separated it from all other parties and rendered its path of duty difficult. From the outset it has resolutely withstood the madness of the war fever, opposing the militarist domination of the civic power, and demanding that the terms of peace shall be stated.[19]

Barclay had in the past been a member of - and subsequently fallen out with – various left wing and anarchist groups in Leicester, and this may in part at least explain his dismissive attitude towards them now.

In parallel with the trade unions, another hugely significant manifestation of the working class desire for self-improvement was the Co-Operative movement. In May 1915 the 47th Annual Co-Operative Congress was held at the De Montfort hall in Leicester, with delegates travelling from across Britain and Ireland to attend. The preamble to the Congress proceedings included a condemnation of

The cover of Leicester ILP Monthly Notes.

Germany and abhorrence of her violation of Belgium. Whilst the tone of the ensuing debate was broadly patriotic, there was some disquiet over payment of war bonuses to workers, for the idea of profiting from war was anathema to many delegates. Some, however, were less equivocal about the righteousness of the war, one delegate:

> …referred to the war as the most cruel that had taken place in all time. He had never thought a war of that kind would come about. It would bring commercial disaster, and it seemed as though no nation would take the responsibility of disorganizing the trade and commerce of the world. But they had to face the difficulty. They were fighting now for small nations; for the sacred rights of international law, and for upholding the weak against the strong.
>
> This was a war for the salvation of the German people as well as for the workers of Europe. After the war they would have to fight for economic freedom and liberty. It was for them, as workers, to be very careful and to watch closely the events that

followed the war. History told them clearly that the workers were the first to suffer from war and the last to recover from it. The middle classes and the governing classes always won the gains accruing from war; they had always taken the advantage and saddled the workers with the cost of war. Therefore it was necessary that they, the workers, should concentrate their efforts upon the Government of their time to see that the cost was put upon those capable of bearing the burden.[20]

The Leicester branch played host and it fell to the Chairman of the Leicester Co-Operative Society, Amos Mann, to make a speech welcoming the delegates. In Mann's view, at this early stage at any rate, the war was merely a temporary interruption in the work of the movement:

Before the terrible conflict in which they were now engaged, the control of industry and how that was to be brought about in order that greater contentment should be the rule in their industrial life, were burning questions. They would be burning questions again when this war was over. Many theories had been advocated and many systems of control presented to the people of this land. All were agreed that the present

Amos Mann, Chairman of the Leicester Co-Operative Society.

system was bad and could not last. It was evident that the system that gave the greatest income to the few and the smallest income to the many stood self-condemned and must perish. Methods of control both violent and peaceful had been suggested - systems which, upon close examination, had in them grave dangers, and the best of which seemed, so far as practical results were concerned, very far off. He suggested that they had object lessons there that day, showing how control of industry could be obtained, which gave immediate benefit to the mass of the workers, and which could be continued to an almost unlimited extent and do no injury, but rather help forward any other practical method of control that the future might set forth.[21]

Mann's views in many areas would lead to him being described as a socialist. He was also President of the Anchor Boot and Shoe

A wounded soldier takes a walk in Victoria Park, Leicester, during the summer of 1915.

Production Society, a workers' co-operative with definite socialist ideals, which had led to the establishment of the Humberstone Garden Suburb. In contrast with Barclay, however, he was also a man of deep religious conviction, being a member of the Church of Christ in Leicester. In this church it was customary for members of the congregation to teach and preach, rather than a minister. The democratic character of the church also influenced Mann's thinking. As the war progressed, his opposition to it would become even more outspoken.

That same month, May 1915, recruiting began for a new unit of artillery raised in Leicester. Tom Crumbie, chairman of Leicester Rugby Football Club, began an appeal for 800 men for the 176th (Leicester) Royal Field Artillery Howitzer Brigade. Crumbie placed the club's ground on Welford Road at the disposal of the Brigade, and the clubhouse became its headquarters. By now young men not in khaki were coming under considerable social pressure to enlist, with government propaganda exhorting women not to be 'selfish' and to relinquish their menfolk to the army. Some women went even further and began giving white feathers (the symbol of cowardice) to men of military age whom they encountered in civilian clothes on the streets. For this reason, the Silver War Badge was instituted, to be worn upon the lapel by those who had seen service and who had been honourably discharged. Likewise, 'On War Service' badges were issued to those on government contract work in industry, and khaki armlets were worn by those who had enlisted into various reserve formations, such as those registered under Lord Derby's scheme, who were told that if they enlisted, they would not be called upon until actually needed. Driver G.E. Cross, one of the so-called 'Tigers Artillery' (as the Leicester Howitzer Brigade was known), had some sympathy with those particular men who were receiving white feathers, despite the fact that they were not of a high enough medical standard to be accepted by the army. In 1915 he penned some verses, which ran:

> God Bless our soldiers and sailors who have come
> From ends of earth to rally, at the beating of the drum.
>
> They hear the bulldog growling as he pulls upon the chain
> And the're [sic] ready to spring with him at the enemy again.
>
> But there's another fellow who can never cross the foam
> He's itching to get at 'em but he's got to stay at home.
>
> If he could only join his pals and prove himself a man
> But no, the doctor's verdict, puts him underneath a ban.
>
> He's often young and eager, and the werefore and the wye, [sic]
> It's sadly unaperent [sic], to the frowning passers by.
>
> He can feel their condemnation, and it takes up all his grit,
> To grin and bear their glances, when he'd like to do his bit.
>
> And so, though some can join the fight, and teach us how to die
> To save the name of England, and keep the Standard high.
>
> Perhaps, if we could read the Hearts, of others we should find
> Full many a saddened Hero, in the man who stayed behind.[22]

However, it was not just the menfolk of Leicester for whom the war offered new opportunities and the chance of travel. For women, too, the war opened their horizons beyond what they might normally have experienced. One of the best examples of this comes in the form of Miss Flora Scott. In 1914 she had been the superintendent of a nursing home in Leicester but, following the outbreak of war, she volunteered to undertake nursing work in Serbia, under trying and difficult conditions. In May 1915 she wrote to a friend back at home, her letter giving a graphic description of the conditions on this front:

> Round Skoplji there are about 3000 Austrian prisoners. These poor fellows, all through this terrible winter, have been sleeping in the basement, cellars and outhouses of an old Turkish barracks, about two miles up in the mountains from Skoplji. Some five or six weeks ago we heard they were dying at the rate of 20 to 30 per day of typhus, with no one to help or go near them. Serbians are terrified of this disease … Two other sisters and I volunteered to go and nurse them. No one could believe, if I told them, the terrible state of those poor men. In one building living and dead were lying together, the living too ill to move, and had not even water for three or four days. Oh! The state of everything – the weather bitterly cold, thick snow, and not even straw to lie on. It was indeed a ghastly business, sorting out living and dead, and more than terrible to see the plight of these poor men.[23]

Nurse Nellie Gilbertson from the Shetland Islands, who undertook a spell of nursing at the 5th Northern General Hospital in Leicester.
(Courtesy of Shetland Museums)

Nevertheless she concluded with the words:

> No one, until they have lived up here, could in any way realize the difficulties one has, and continually I have asked myself: Is it doing a scrap of good to stay here? Then when I go into a ward and see their faces light up, and hear them say in their Austrian language, "Sister, a drink," I feel I must stay … I love being here, and I cannot imagine there is a more beautifully situated place in the world.[24]

On the home front, women would find it harder, at least initially, to get society to accept that they had a role to play. That summer the *Leicester Daily Mercury* commented:

> The practice of employing women in the Postal Service as clerks and to deliver letters has not yet been adopted in Leicester. Women are not being employed as drivers and conductors on tramcars as this is not seen as a suitable occupation for women.[25]

However, other towns were beginning to employ women as conductors on their tramways, and Leicester would follow suit before the end of 1915. Women were to become an increasingly common sight, working in many different industries and trades. As well as donning overalls in munitions and engineering factories, they could now be found working for example in banks as cashiers and as booking clerks at the railway stations (with lower class women undertaking the dirtier tasks as engine and carriage cleaners in the sheds). At the Goodwin Barsby engineering works, Pochin records that:

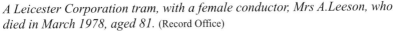

A Leicester Corporation tram, with a female conductor, Mrs A.Leeson, who died in March 1978, aged 81. (Record Office)

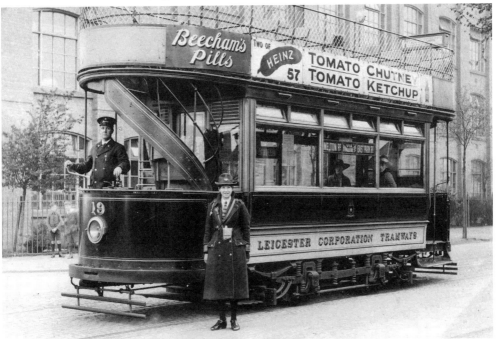

Female tramways staff in Leicester. (Record Office)

...the thin trickle of younger men into the Forces [continued] until the situation became so acute that, for the first time in the company's history, women were engaged to take their place ... it was on [shell production] that the first female labour was employed, but very soon girls were replacing men in the offices. Edith Record was the first, coming as a clerk to the general office in May 1915 ... Nowadays, it is strange to think how the innovation of female labour and staff was resented by the wives of the men who worked with them. Frank Pochin used to tell of very heated interviews with irate females who considered their husband's affections in jeopardy.[26]

In the Leicester textile industries there had always been a large proportion of female employees, and it was a natural progression for women in these industries to take on the work of men, although generally speaking the men's machinery was heavier and harder to operate. By the end of the year an agreement had been reached between the Leicester textiles unions and the Leicestershire Masters' Associations, under which women were admitted:

…upon certain operations hitherto ordinarily restricted to male labour [provided that these operations were such as they were] physically fit to perform, [and that they were paid] the same rates of wages as are now paid to males for an equivalent quantity of work.[27]

Through the summer of 1915, recruiting rallies were held across Leicester in an effort to make up for the perceived tardiness of her response to the war when it first broke out. At each of the rallies there were a number of speakers but the biggest draw was always Private William Buckingham VC. At many of the rallies, whilst politicians occupied the platform, Buckingham would move quietly among the

IN LOVING MEMORY OF

Private W. Buckingham

Leicester's **V.C.** Hero,

Who was killed in action September 15th, 1916, somewhere in France.

HE WON THE VICTORIA CROSS for conspicuous acts of bravery and devotion to duty in rescuing and rendering aid to the wounded whilst exposed to heavy fire, especially at Neuve Chapelle, on 10th and 12th March

An in memoriam card, honouring Private William Buckingham VC.

MEN OF LEICESTER
WHY STOP HERE
WHEN YOUR CHUMS ARE OUT THERE?

LINE UP NOW.

TO - NIGHT (WEDNESDAY),

THE MEETINGS ARE AT

Overton Road Bridge at 7.45.

Corner of Green Lane Road & Harewood St. at 9

Private Buckingham, V.C., will be there

YOUNG WOMEN OF LEICESTER
WOULDN'T YOU LIKE
TO SEE
YOUR "BEST BOY" IN KHAKI!

YOU COULD BE PROUD OF HIM THEN.

PRIVATE BUCKINGHAM, V.C.
WILL BE AT THE MEETINGS

TO-NIGHT (THURSDAY),

AT

Corner of Mantle Rd. & Battenburg Rd. at 7.45.

Corner of Rowan Street & Beatrice Road at 9.

Flyers for Leicester recruiting meetings attended by William Buckingham VC. Often Buckingham would move quietly among the crowd, whilst others spoke from the platform.

assembled crowd, wearing his VC, and stopping here and there to chat to lads of military age. His value to recruiting was undoubtedly enormous, but eventually, with his wounds fully healed, Buckingham tired of the notoriety and asked to return to active service. He would lose his life on the Somme the following year, but his example and his efforts to inspire them seem to have had the desired effect upon the young men of Leicester. The second part of the *Leicester War Souvenir* magazine, produced that summer, reported under the heading *Leicester and Recruiting*:

> The state of affairs in regard to recruiting in Leicester is happily much more satisfactory than during January and February, and, apparently the "eligible" young men of the town are becoming reconciled to the fact that it is men the country requires at the present moment. The controversy in connection with the lack of recruits locally has been rather painful, and it would no doubt have cleared the air to a great extent if those young men who had been rejected had been able to wear a badge or some distinctive sign to show that they had submitted themselves for enlistment. Then again, the enormous amount of Government work that has been produced in Leicester must have had its effect in keeping men at home who otherwise may have joined the forces, and in these cases also it is not fair that workers upon important Government contracts should be placed upon the list of so-called "shirkers".[28]

In September 1915, Leicester raised its last battalion for active service, the 11th (Service) Battalion Leicestershire Regiment (Midland Pioneers). Wearing a distinctive crossed rifle and pick badge on their collar, the men were part of a unit which was raised both to be able to fight as infantry but also construct roads, trenches and field fortifications. Crumbie again was instrumental in helping to raise the battalion, which undertook its early training on the Tigers' ground. It was also presented with a monkey as a mascot by Miss Flora

Company Sergeant Major George Henry Birch, of the 11th Leicesters.

Inside the former tramways depot on Belgrave Gate, now turned over to shell production. This is a view of the belt-driven lathes.

Scott, who had by now returned from Serbia, though how and where she obtained such a creature remains obscure.

That same month Leicester delivered its first completed batch of artillery shells to the Government. It is believed that these were the first 4.5" Howitzer shells delivered by any firm which had not been engaged in munitions production prior to the outbreak of war. Leicester's contribution towards the mobilization of industry towards the war effort (which was one of the key factors in Britain's victory in the conflict) was an extraordinary one. In early 1915, the shortage of artillery shells for the army became a political scandal, the government having before the war obtained its shells mainly from Woolwich Arsenal and a few private contractors, which were now unable to cope with the demand. In response, the government had indicated that it was prepared to compulsorily remove trained engineers from private firms and install them in newly built munitions factories; but a group of Leicester firms came together and insisted that there was a better way. The removal of their workers and the disruption that this would cause, they argued, would be counter-productive. Instead they offered to turn their own factories and employees over to munitions work, working together to overcome any shortcomings which they might individually have had in terms of machinery.

This co-operative arrangement was so successful that it set a pattern which was emulated in other parts of Britain. In the official account of Leicester's munitions work, under the heading *An Experiment in Engineering Co-Operation,* is recorded:

> When the history of Leicester and District Engineering Trade is written, no brighter chapter will be found than the one dealing with the part employers and employees played in the Great War. Without experience, and without time in which to gain experience, they were called upon at a moment of crisis to help in the supply of ammunition to the Allied forces. Indeed, they were pioneers in the great movement for the manufacture of high explosive shells, which spread throughout the country early in 1915 ... Major-General Mahon, who represented the War Office, had grave doubts as to their ability to do the work. In his opinion, shells could only be made properly after many years' experience ... but the employers stood firm. [They] saw no difficulty in the way of local manufacture, provided the different firms were willing to pool their resources. By division of work into processes, the manufacture of shells might be carried out by the firms in the district.[29]

A depot was provided for the collection and storage of, as well as the finishing processes for, ammunition by using a Leicester Tramways Department building on Belgrave Gate. Later production included 6" high explosive projectiles and also 6" gas shells. Lest it be thought that the citizens of Leicester were exposed to extreme danger by this work being carried out so close to residential areas, it must be stressed that the actual filling of shells with TNT and other explosive materials does not appear to have taken place in the town. Only the machining of the casings was undertaken and these were then shipped to establishments such as the National Shell Filling Factory at Chilwell, in nearby Nottinghamshire, to be filled. Nonetheless, the work in Leicester was not without challenges. The history continues:

The Hohenzollern Redoubt, a formidable German defensive position where many Leicester soldiers in the county's territorial battalions met their end in 1915.

They were confronted with many problems. The first was the method of dividing and standardizing the manufacture of High Explosive Shells in the works of the different firms comprising the group. The plant and tools in many instances were rough and ill-adapted for the accurate operations required. The lathes were classified, jigs and gauges obtained, and high speed steel boring cutters and other special tools procured. Working limits had to be ascertained by experiment and modified by experience.[30]

The shells which Leicester was now producing were desperately needed, as at the end of September the BEF launched a major offensive at Loos, in co-ordination with the French army's assault in Artois. The pattern was now becoming familiar – initial surprise meant that the British managed to penetrate the German line and advanced some distance into the enemy's reserve positions. However, exhaustion on the part of the attacking troops, combined with the arrival of German reinforcements, brought the offensive to a halt. One of the hardest German positions to capture had been the formidable Hohenzollern Redoubt, a strongpoint bristling with machine guns, set amid the German lines immediately in front of Corons de Maroc. On 13 October 1915, the 1st/4th Leicesters were allotted the task of capturing it. The preliminary bombardment was weak and German machine gunners were well prepared – as always. Despite the bravery of the men involved, the attack was a disaster. It took a week for news of the fate which had overtaken so many local men to filter back to Leicester, but on 20 October the *Mercury* reported:

> It is with profound regret that we have to confirm the rumours that have been so persistently in circulation the last few days, that the 1st/4th Leicesters have suffered severe losses. The battalion was in action on October 13, and how they suffered may be judged from the list of officers whose deaths have been officially notified to their relatives. The receipt of the news yesterday caused a painful sensation in the town, and the sympathy of all will go out to the relatives of those who have fallen. It is impossible at present to obtain anything like a complete list of casualties among non-commissioned officers and men.[31]

It was probably the hardest single blow which hit the town in four years of war; although other battalions of the regiment would be grievously mauled in the years which lay ahead, they were raised from across the county, and only the 1st/4th drew its recruits so narrowly from within the borough. In the weeks which followed, more details of what had happened to Leicester's soldiers began to emerge. Letters from survivors began to appear in local papers, describing the battle in candid terms. One, from a Lance Corporal Richard Pexton, read:

Private Len Richards, 1st/4th Leicesters, of 35 Danvers Road. A battalion signaller, he was killed in action at the Hohenzollern Redoubt.

> A small ration of rum was handed round, and then a message "The CO wishes God-speed and good luck to all his men." Officers stood, watch in hand, counting the crawling seconds. "Five minutes to two, Four! Three! Two! One!" – then, "Over

you go with the best of luck." Brave lads, up they climbed at intervals of a yard apart liberating a heavy mist of smoke as they went. A few seconds and the next line followed, and we advanced straight to our front through the smoke and suddenly came out into the light of day – and Hell. The spit and phut of the rifles and of machine gun bullets was incessant, incredible but the boys never wavered. Men fell and lay where they fell, but the long thin line went forward, determined and strong.[32]

On 29 October the *Mercury* carried an anonymous letter from a survivor of the action. Headed *Return from the Battle*, it illustrates the confusion and chaos of the fight, but also the resilience of those who had survived:

Saturday night, and the boys are reading the papers from home, and the mail is full of requests for news of missing sons and husbands. Quite a number of letters are from various hospitals in England and Scotland, even from some of the men we thought had gone under. May there be many more such. They all write cheerfully and express the hope that they will soon recover. Would I could paint a picture of the scene as the boys came back from the fight. The only spectators were two or three NCOs who had gone ahead to prepare the sleeping accommodation, and get some hot tea ready for them. They were led back by the surviving officers, Captain Jarvis and Lieut Ball, and it was dusk as they swung into the yard where our stores are situated. Some had smoke helmets on their heads, because they had lost their caps in the charge, and their earliest questions were concerning comrades who were known to have been hit. Had

Private Thomas Bottoms, killed in action at the Hohenzollern Redoubt in October 1915. Previously a foundry hand with Richards of Martin Street, he and his family lived at 144 Surrey Street, Leicester.

we seen any of them, or did we know if they had gone to hospital. Not much was said, but a real handshake was silent testimony to our pleasure at seeing comrades once more. They could not give much news of others less fortunate than themselves, because as they stood in the trenches they only saw just the fellows in their vicinity. As no trench is straight, it is impossible to see many at one time, and going across the open was no time for looking about, except for looking for the enemy. All were loud in praise of their leaders, and numerous were the instances of the pluck of various NCOs and men.[33]

The butt plate of a Lee Enfield rifle, found recently at the site of the Hohenzollern Redoubt. Stamped '4 Leic', it would have been issued at the Magazine in 1914, and belonged to a Leicester soldier who probably lost his life in 1915.

Some of the wounded from the Hohenzollern Redoubt battle would have been fortunate enough to have been treated in one of the Leicester war hospitals or convalescent homes. Indeed wounded soldiers would have been very much in the consciousness of the Leicester public; the Snow brothers, for example, playing cricket on the recreation ground across the Saffron Lane from their home, could see the trains with large red crosses painted upon the carriages, full of heavily bandaged soldiers, waiting on the Midland Railway viaduct to enter the town. The wounded received much sympathy and hospitality from local people. Constance Garner remembered:

I was born and lived until my 12th birthday in a cottage situated in that part of Northampton Street, which was pulled down to make way for the extension of Charles Street from Church Street to London Road. One of the excitements for children in that area was to run down Charles Street to its junction with Rutland Street when they heard the fire bell ring to watch the horses taking the firemen to the fire as quickly as they could ... Another thrill during the early part of the 1914-1918 war was to go to the back of the station in Campbell Street and cheer the ambulances which brought the wounded soldiers to the hospitals in the area.[34]

As the war progressed, the 5th Northern General Hospital became the administrative centre for a number of other hospitals and convalescent homes in the town and surrounding district. The North Evington War Hospital, formerly the Poor Law Union Infirmary (and latterly known as the City General Hospital) was one such satellite. Mary Thornley of Evington Street remembered providing hospitality for the wounded, like many other middle class families:

> ...in the First World War, my mother and grandmother used to visit the soldiers at North Evington War Hospital which ... is the General Hospital now, it was an Infirmary place before the war I think. In the First World War it was quite a big hospital and we used to walk there from Evington Street, straight through down to Melbourne Road, up Derwent Street to Mere Road, down Parkvale Road which is at the side of Spinney Hill, cross over and you are at the corner of Gwendolen Road, walk up Gwendolen Road and you're at the hospital main gates. They used to go every Thursday and Saturday or every Thursday and Sunday I think. I used to go sometimes with them and then one or two of the men if they were well enough to get away were allowed to come and have tea and one of the nurses came with

Wounded soldiers are unloaded from a train at Leicester's Midland Station for transfer to hospital. (Record Office)

them once or twice. I remember one man he came from
Nottingham and his name was Waterson, it's funny how you
remember these names isn't it? And then there was an Australian
soldier who visited them after he had been back to Australia and
he came to see them after when he came to England again. That
was all from the First World War but they certainly had these
men in their blue suits with their red ties, they wore flannel like
suits.[35]

Whilst visiting wounded soldiers was undoubtedly a visible and
obvious way for the middle classes to express their patriotic duty, that
does not mean to say that the comfort and cheer offered to the casualties
was unappreciated, indeed quite the opposite was true. One wounded
tommy, Private Arthur Allday of the Queen's Regiment, wrote an open
letter in the visiting book of Miss Gladys Forryan, a 23-year-old school
teacher, who lived at 106 Howard Road, Clarendon Park, just a short
distance from the 5th Northern General Hospital, and who also was a
regular visitor in 1915:

Wounded soldiers and nurses at North Evington War Hospital, Leicester.

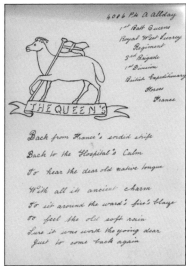

Pages from the autograph book of Gladys Forryan, who visited wounded soldiers at the 5th Northern General Hospital in Leicester. (Courtesy of Tony Walne)

I hope you will forgive me for taking so much space in your book but I can't resist the temptation of writing on this page my sincerest thanks to the People of Leicester for their great kindness. I am sure the month I have spent here under rather sad circumstances has been made joyful by everybody's kindness … I shall be going back to London shortly and I know I shall take with me everybody's Good Wishes. Can I say more Leicester, will I never forget their goodness?[36]

The various war hospitals in Leicester drew out the best in the communities surrounding them. The 1st Troop of Leicester Girl Guides was formed during the First World War and the girls undertook duties at the various hospitals, as well as helping at the wounded soldiers' waiting room at the Midland Station. A Leicester firm, Dryad, provided off-cuts of cane from its wicker furniture to the hospitals for use in basket making by wounded soldiers; an early form of occupational therapy. The founder of Dryad, Harry Peach, would go on to be a significant figure in the Arts and Crafts movement in Britain during the First World War. The production of Dryad's cane furniture,

Leicester bank clerks, undertaking voluntary munitions work on Sundays, in the 'shell shop' at Standard Engineering Works in 1915. (Record Office)

however, was halted as the war progressed, and instead the firm began producing shell, gun and balloon baskets, as well as aircraft nose-cones, for Vickers-Armstrong and the War Office.

One of the reasons for which wounded soldiers wore 'hospital blue' was in order to make them conspicuous as such, for a persistent problem during the war – in Leicester as much as anywhere – was the 'treating' of wounded soldiers. Well-meaning civilians naturally felt inclined to show their appreciation for what the wounded had been through by buying them drinks in pubs, but there were cases of drunkenness as a result. For this reason it was actually illegal under the Defence of the Realm Act of 1914 to buy wounded soldiers alcohol; this would not be the only area of public life into which 'DORA' (as it was nicknamed) would pry. The Act soon became a catch-all which gave the government sweeping powers.

Whilst the war had curtailed the activities of Leicester Rugby Football Club, and the county cricket club ground at Aylestone Road was used for military training purposes, association football continued at Filbert Street during the war, albeit in a reduced form. The 1914/15 season had been allowed to continue as planned, but this decision had attracted harsh criticism from some quarters that a contest far more serious than mere football was taking place across the Channel, and it was felt that this was the one in which sportsmen should be playing their part. Thus for the new season, which opened in the autumn of 1915, Leicester Fosse found themselves playing not in the Football League, as previously, but in the much-reduced Midland Section of the Regional League. With railway capacity at a premium due to the movement of troops and munitions, confining football to local derbies in this way meant that it was not necessary to accommodate large numbers of travelling away supporters each Saturday afternoon.

This was not the only change brought about in football by the war; there were now to be no cups played for, and players would receive no wages, only out of pocket expenses. League points were also suspended for the duration. Fosse were even forced to change their playing strip from dark blue jerseys to blue and white stripes, due to the shortage of blue dye caused by the war. Matches were compulsorily reduced to eighty minutes duration, but during a home fixture with Bradford City

Wounded soldiers from Leicester hospitals enjoying a picnic at Bradgate House, courtesy of Mr Thomas Everard of the famous Leicestershire brewing family. July 1915.

on 4 December 1915, weather conditions were so bad that a Leicester Fosse match was foreshortened at the referee's discretion to just seventy three minutes, with no half-time break.

Thus ended a year which had witnessed unprecedented changes in the lives of the citizens of Leicester. Probably in no other era of the town's history had so much changed, and so quickly, but the war was yet to reach its zenith and more heartache and grief was to lie in store.

Samuel Dennis, a schoolteacher who played for Leicester YMCA Football Club. During the First World War he joined the Leicestershire Regiment, commissioned as a Second Lieutenant.

CHAPTER 3

Do all you can

The year of 1916 would see the First World War intensify, as the Allied nations resolved to increase the pressure on the Central Powers by mounting simultaneous offensives on all major fronts. The forces of Great Britain were now beginning to come into their stride, with the many thousands of men who had volunteered in 1914 now adequately trained and beginning to reach the battlefields in numbers that could make a difference. It was the Western Front which would see the greatest of these offensives that summer, but the year began with dramatic developments in a more obscure theatre of conflict.

In 1914, the entry of Turkey into the war on Germany's side (together with that of Japan alongside the Allies at around the same time) had made it a truly global, rather than merely a European,

Captured Turkish guns in Basra, Mesopotamia, early 1916.

conflict. It was the threat that Turkey now presented to oil supplies in Mesopotamia (modern Iraq) which led British forces into action there, in order to protect them. However, through a series of misadventures, by early 1916 the army corps under Major General Townshend found itself besieged in Kut-al-Amara, a small town on the River Tigris. A relief force was urgently assembled, which included the 2nd Battalion Leicestershire Regiment. In January that year they fought two bitter battles with the Turks, at Sheikh Sa'ad and at the Wadi. Both were inconclusive, with heavy casualties sustained. In this flat, open country, Turkish bullets were as lethal as German ones were in France when soldiers left cover to advance. In April 1916 a soldier named William Billings, a reinforcement from Weymouth Street, off Belgrave Road in Leicester, found himself in this hot, barren, inhospitable land, preparing for another attempt to break through to Kut. He kept a diary, part of which describes his experiences at the Battle of Sannaiyat:

Wednesday April 5: Bombardment begun at 4.55 and the attack is being successfully carried the first line being taken without a casualty, second and third trenches taken after. The bombardment and attack lasted about 2 hours. This is the right flank position. At 2.15 we [are] pushed forward about 5 miles, this being all entrenched by the Turks but captured very easily. We are still on reserve. We marched away about 5.30 and stopped again about 8 o'clock where we were told to get a bit of sleep.

William Billings, of Weymouth Street, Leicester. He arrived in Mesopotamia as reinforcement for the 2nd Battalion Leicestershire Regiment in 1916.

Thursday April 6: We marched away about 12 o'clock intending to make a charge with surprise but owing to some mistake it was daylight before we got near the Turkish position so we got a very good reception, myself being wounded by shrapnel.[1]

Following the battles of Sheik Sa'ad, the Wadi and now Sannaiyat, Leicester newspapers would carry portrait photographs of many more local men who had fallen on these faraway battlefields in an ultimately unsuccessful attempt to reach the force at Kut.

Across Great Britain, the way of life of the British people was changed for ever that spring with the passing of the 1916 Summer Time Act, which meant that, for the first time, on 21 May that year, clocks went forward one hour. The main reason for the move was to assist the war effort by enabling those in agriculture to make the maximum use of daylight. Most of the people of Leicester took the novelty of the move to 'daylight saving time' in their stride, though the *Leicester Mail* reported that a few found the new time difficult to adjust to:

> At least one Leicester man was so intent upon observing the law that he forgot to wind the clock up after putting the hands to "summer time" with the result that the clock stopped at 4am! Another Leicester man confessed yesterday that he altered his clock all right before going to bed, and that on getting up he forgot that he had done so and put it forward another hour, after which he hastened to keep a 9 o'clock appointment and was on the spot at 8am – new time. The children's bedtime last evening arrived all too soon for the little ones, and with daylight lasting up to nearly 10pm parents found the difficulty of getting their offspring into the mood for sleep was one of the greatest drawbacks to the new regime.[2]

HMS Defence, *lost at the Battle of Jutland in 1916.* (Courtesy of Joyce Billings)

The early summer of 1916 also brought developments on the naval front. Since the outbreak of war, the British public had been eagerly anticipating a 'second Trafalgar', when the Royal Navy would sweep the German High Seas Fleet from the sea. For two years little had happened, apart from a frustrating stalemate. This however was a war of blockade rather than open confrontation, with the German fleet perceived by the Kaiser as too valuable to risk in an all out fight. The British too were cautious; their commander Admiral Jellicoe was described as 'the only man on either side who could lose the war in an afternoon'. So much did Britain's security depend upon her control of the seas. Then, in May, came news that the German ships had left their bases and put to sea. It was a trap, designed to lure the faster British battlecruisers away from the heavier battleships, and destroy them in isolation. For two days in the North Sea, off the coast of Jutland, the two mighty fleets traded shells in a running fight. The result was

Signal Boy Herbert William Garton, of Hawthorn Street, Leicester, lost aboard HMS Defence at the Battle of Jutland.
(Courtesy of Joyce Billings)

inconclusive, with both sides claiming victory. The German fleet had not been swept from the seas by the British, but neither had it achieved anything significant. The High Seas Fleet had assaulted its jailer, said Winston Churchill, but it remained in jail. Yet when the great clash eventually came, which proved to be indecisive, there was confusion and frustration, not to mention disappointment, among many on the home front.

Leicester sailors were in the thick of the action. At least six Leicester men were aboard HMS *Queen Mary* and lost their lives when she was sunk. Other local men were lost aboard HMS *Invincible* and HMS *Defence*. One survivor of HMS *Warrior*, Stoker 1st Class J.A. Critchlow of 94 Hazel Street, Leicester, was granted leave in the aftermath of the battle, and when interviewed at home by a journalist, sought to correct public perceptions of the battle. The reporter stated that he:

...found him looking hale and hearty, and apparently none the worse for his experiences. Like many sailors, he declined to talk battle, except in very general terms. He was astounded, he said, on reaching England, to see the gloomy look on the faces of many people. Some seemed to have the impression that the British suffered a defeat but instead of that the Navy had achieved a great victory, as the country should someday learn. Turning to the action itself, he expressed pride in the manner in which his ship acquitted itself in the action. Her life was short, for she was in the thick of the fray and heavily shelled by the Germans, but before she sank she severely punished the enemy craft. When riddled she continued to use the guns, and did so as long as it was possible. The loss of life was small in comparison with the dangers that were run. When in distress the *Warrior* appealed for assistance, and a ship came along, took her in tow, and eventually rescued the crew … shortly before the men were rescued the waves were washing the ship's deck, and when all had safely landed on the rescue ship the crew gave three lusty cheers for the *Warrior*.[3]

Four other Leicester men, Stoker Petty Officer Tilley, Ship's Corporal Whitaker, Private B.F. Tyler Royal Marines, and Able Seaman Hadden were also rescued from this vessel.

For three months now the 1916 Military Service Act had been in force. The Act introduced conscription for the first time in British history, and all fit males were now deemed eligible for military service. The Act allowed for exemptions on the grounds of an occupation vital to the war effort, in situations where call-up would result in severe economic hardship to those dependents left behind, or on medical grounds. The fourth and most controversial category was for those who had a conscientious objection to military service and the taking of human life. Some Leicester men accepted conscription stoically; James Drake, for example, remembered:

…as I had already joined the St John's Ambulance Brigade, I was ready and eager when I was called up at eighteen to join the Sick Berth Reserve of the Royal Navy. I received my calling-up papers at 5 o'clock when I was at work, and ordered to report to Devonport the next morning.[4]

Others who could have claimed exemption through essential war work chose to enlist anyway. Belgrave-born Harry Halford remembered many years later how his work producing military uniforms might have kept him away from the battlefield:

> I was on khaki at Hart & Levi, and I was exempt from military work, but any road I took it in me head one morning and I went and joined up … I felt as though I should go, all my friends were going, I thought its time I went…[5]

Halford joined the Royal Field Artillery and was to see active service in France. Others, who objected to killing but none the less wished to serve their country, could appeal against military service, and in most cases were allocated non-combatant roles. Herbert Arnesby Orton, a clerk in a Leicester drapery shop, remembered:

Alexander Patrick, a tailor who worked at Corah's in Leicester. As he was working on military uniforms, his was a reserved occupation.
(Courtesy of Alison Coates)

> I was a young man … I played rugby football, and did all the general things that a young man would do … and then the war broke out …. Well I didn't feel that the sort of thing I wanted to do was stick a bayonet through somebody, so what I did was join the Royal Army Medical Corps … I was called up and I had to make a decision, whether I was going to join the fighting forces. I didn't, I joined the medical corps.[6]

Men who wished to be exempted from military service on whatever grounds had to appear before a local tribunal, which usually consisted of several prominent businessmen and politicians together with a military representative. In July 1916 the Leicester Tribunal, held at the Town Hall, consisted of Alderman A. Sawday presiding, supported by Alderman Russell Frears, Mr J.B. Everard, and Mr Charles Bennion of British United Shoe Machinery. Colonel Bruxner-Randall was the military representative. A typical session from around this time covered three sons of a furniture remover, of whom the eldest was granted conditional exemption providing one of the other brothers enlisted; a tailor, who had already been granted six months grace, was awarded a further month; whilst the manager of a one-man travelling business with an epileptic father and a mother with heart disease was also given a conditional exemption.

In all cases of conditional exemption, the men were required to join Leicester's Volunteer Training Corps; with the coming of conscription, the government had finally decided to take these ad hoc formations in hand, and across Britain these men were now placed under the 1863 Volunteer Act, as a means of regulating their terms of service. It was not until later in the year that the government belatedly placed them under the auspices of the County Territorial Association, but by this time much damage had been done. A Mr Hull, of the Leicester VTC, described the lax attitude in the corps. His company

Charles Bennion, managing director of British United Shoe Machinery in Leicester.

had now dwindled to platoon strength. The fall in numbers was attributable to the age limit for active service being recently raised, with the added consequence that the men left behind in offices and factories were now forced to work longer hours, giving them less free time for drill. There was also a general feeling of disappointment that the efforts of the Volunteers were perceived neither as useful nor valuable by the authorities, and the obvious lack of equipment could be taken as evidence of this. Major W.G.S. Rolleston, a company commander in the Leicester corps, reported that his men were:

So ill-armed that it is not worth talking about.[7]

Although some obsolete rifles had trickled through since the government's acceptance of the Volunteers, among those of Rolleston's men that were armed the predominant weapon was the shotgun. Little more than half the force had a uniform of any kind, and none had a proper overcoat. As the wrangling over who would provide these continued, the War Office settled upon a scheme whereby a uniform would be provided to a man once he had proved himself 'efficient' (to use the War Office terminology). Two things mitigated against this, the

You are warned to bring your National Registration Card, Armlet and Army Form W 3194 (White Card) with you when reporting at Glen Parva Barracks.

Army Form W. 3195.

NOTICE PAPER to be sent to each man who has been attested and transferred to the Army Reserve under the provisions of the Royal Warrant of the 20th October, 1915.

[This Notice Paper should be despatched so that it will reach the addressee at least 14 clear days before he is required to present himself at the appointed place.

In accordance with the provisions of Section 24 (2) of the Reserve Forces Act, 1882, "evidence of the delivery at the last registered place of abode of a man belonging to the Army Reserve of a ... , or of a letter addressed to such man, and containing a notice, shall be evidence that such notice was brought to the knowledge of such man."]

Surname _Ward_

Christian Name _Alfred_

Address _37 Laxton St._

Leicester

Number as shown on the Card, Army Form W. 3194 } _71_

Group Number _8._

You are hereby warned that you will be required to rejoin for service with the Colours on the _10th February_ 1916.

You should therefore present yourself at _Glen Parva Barracks_ on the above date, not later than _9-15 a.m._ o'clock, bringing this paper with you.

A Railway Warrant is enclosed herewith.*

*This will be struck out if the man resides within 3 miles of the place at which he is required to present himself.

2nd February Date.

TOWN HALL _Leicester_ Place.

J. H. Clark Signature.

Lieut. Rank.

_M. O._ Appointment.

A call-up paper from February 1916. This is for a Leicester man who had previously enlisted voluntarily in the Army Reserve; but many more unwilling recruits would shortly receive similar notices.

first being lack of equipment, which hampered training, and the second being that, with the coming of conscription, men were forced to join by tribunals as a condition of exemption. Thus they were not true Volunteers in the old sense of the word, and frequently exemption was only temporary and so the men were not enrolled long enough to qualify as 'efficient' before they left.

Conscription however had more serious consequences in society as a whole. The bottom line now was that for the first time, those who for religious, political or other reasons could not support Britain's part in the war would come into direct confrontation with the state. Although the Military Service Act clearly allowed for conscientious objection, men expressing such views would be vilified and, in the minds of many members of the public, equated with cowards.

Although they were out of step with the overwhelming weight of public opinion, many of these men showed great courage in holding on to their principles and beliefs in spite of the harsh treatment that they received as a result. The members of the tribunals were frequently prejudiced against them, and also often ignorant of the finer points of the law in these cases. In Leicester in particular, there existed a strong evangelical pacifist tradition which clashed head-on with the generally pro-military bias of the tribunals. In April 1916, seven young men belonging to the Church of Christ sought total exemption from military service, and were supported in this by Amos Mann, who had been a member for forty years and was now an elder. Mann told one tribunal that:

> When [I] was a young man, if a member joined the forces, he would have been dealt with by the church ... almost every preacher and teacher amongst us has declared war to be contrary to the teaching of Christ, and ... many of our churches have even separated young men from their fellowship for joining the military forces.[8]

Religious objectors outnumbered those with political motives by about three to one across Britain as a whole; the latter group usually received even less recognition from the tribunals than the former. Even if they accepted that the objector was genuine in his beliefs, then the only compromise on offer was non-combatant service, which was still under military control. The so-called 'absolutists' would not entertain this, and pressed for absolute exemption. Usually they received prison sentences of up to two years.

Horace Gladstone Twilley was a partner in Vestry Street Mills, a textile firm in Leicester. The son of working class Radical parents, he was a socialist and was also the secretary of the Leicester branch of

Conscientious objectors from the Leicester Church of Christ serving their sentence at Dartmoor prison. (Record Office)

the No-Conscription Fellowship. After his tribunal, at which he claimed absolute exemption, he was arrested in May 1916. Although he was allowed home briefly upon payment of £20 bail, he was re-arrested on 1 June 1916. His brother Fred, already in the army, was concerned for the effect that his stance would have, both on Horace and upon their mother. He wrote to his wife:

> Am very worried about Horace this morning as this is the day that he goes up and likely goes to prison or military detention. It is a great source of worry to mother. I don't know just how we shall do if he is taken … I have spoken to the paymaster about that allowance matter and he says if Horace is placed so as not to be able to look after her, he will try and get it fixed up. Even if Horace gets off, which is improbable, the notice his case is receiving will injure his business and make it bad for both him and his partner.[9]

Twilley was taken to Glen Parva Barracks at Wigston, and subjected to some rough treatment from the soldiers. A sergeant there told him that they would break his spirit, and he was dragged to and from the parade ground as the soldiers tried to force him to wear khaki, which he refused to do. The brutal treatment led other conscientious objectors to call for a doctor to attend, but he passed Twilley as fit. However word of his mistreatment had reached his Congregational Church and the minister, also a pacifist, attempted to intervene on his behalf. His brother's appeal to Ramsay MacDonald for help fell upon deaf ears, for MacDonald was by this stage in the war if not exactly supporting the conflict, at least adopting a more mainstream position, much to the chagrin of the ILP and others on the left.

Charlie Hassell, a Leicester conscientious objector who was imprisoned for his anti-war stance. (Courtesy of Gillian Lighton)

After twenty eight days at Glen Parva, Twilley was transferred to a prison cell at Richmond Castle in North Yorkshire. Here he was visited by Mabel Thompson of the No-Conscription Fellowship, who wrote afterwards:

I had an interesting conversation with Mr Twilling [sic], Secretary of the Leicester NCF who asked me to pass on the idea of the value of concentrated thought being directed towards our friends in prison at a certain time. He had felt a strange power at such times. For instance he knew that at eleven o'clock that morning friends in Leicester were all thinking of and praying for him and the sense of power was unspeakable. 'In ordinary times', said Mr Twilling, 'we only think of our friends occasionally, we are too busy. But at a time like this much thought is coming our way constantly and it reaches us in our imprisonment.'[10]

Twilley also wrote to his brother Fred, thanking him for his efforts in trying to get him out of prison, telling him:

The worst is over now, I believe. I have had a fairly easy time here ... I am afraid I must await developments. In any case do not worry. Everything may turn out all right in due course. [I am] out of the cells now [and] quartered in a house with seven other COs [awaiting court martial].[11]

On 15 July, he received 112 days imprisonment, and after time spent at Durham jail he would be transferred to Wormwood Scrubs in London. The same day that his sentence was passed, many miles away in France, fellow Leicester men were battling for their lives at the height of the Somme offensive. The four Leicestershire battalions, which had been raised in 1914 as part of Kitchener's Army, now formed the 110th Infantry Brigade. Although they had been in France for almost a year, their first real taste of battle was to come on the Somme, in the attack on the Bazentin Ridge, which had started in the early hours of 14 July. All four battalions went into action together, fighting their way through the dense undergrowth of Bazentin Wood. A clerk in a Leicester hosiery factory before the war, Private Douglas Bacon was serving with the headquarters of the 9th Battalion at this battle. He wrote afterwards:

Private Bertram Richards, of the 8th Battalion Leicestershire Regiment. He served on the Somme in 1916.

Being our first experience of assault, we were naturally excited and expectant, and apart from the infernal noise and smoke, and the chilly air of the morning, we were not uncomfortable. The Battn Sgt Major, to uphold the honour of his rank, had bethought himself fit to fill his waterbottle with rum – how and where he got it remains a mystery but a share was very acceptable ... [with] one continual roar of guns and shells whistling and shrieking through the air – talk was impossible – it was a perfect avalanche of destruction, and how any Boche could have been alive to withstand the infantry attack was beyond comprehension.[12]

Bacon continued:

The Headquarters crouched, as the others, in shell holes or trenches, from which could be seen the troops of the attacking battalions moving forward in extended order at a walking pace ... by that time most of the enemy machine guns had been silenced, though one or two, more lucky or more persevering than the rest, blazed away in solitude and desperation, and deserving the Iron Cross, it is to be hoped they received it![13]

The Bazentin Ridge battle, although marked by initial success, with the Leicestershire Brigade taking all of its objectives, wrought terrible destruction in their ranks. The casualty returns were appallingly high, and through that summer long lists of wounded and killed appeared in the Leicester newspapers, together with photographs and poignant obituaries of those who had been killed. For yet another time in this war, Leicester was hit hard, with black drapes at the windows of many a terraced house, indicating the loss of a dearly loved son, brother or father.

Lieutenant Jimmy Burdett, the son of the manager of Lloyds Bank in Leicester. He fought on the Somme with the 6th Leicesters.

The First World War witnessed many new technical advances, spurred on by military necessity. Both the tank and the aeroplane were to make an impact on the battlefield that summer, but both were as yet imperfect and unpredictable, and often as likely to injure their crew as the enemy. Aeroplanes in particular killed as many young pilots in training as died in aerial combat with the enemy. One such young man, who lost his life in an accident without ever having flown operationally, was Second Lieutenant Charles Carryer, the son of a hosiery factory owner of Leicester. He was serving with No.5 Reserve Squadron Royal Flying Corps, when he lost his life on 13 August 1916. A report stated:

> The inquest on Acting-Flight-Commander Charles Ivan Carryer, the victim of the shocking air tragedy, which occurred near Gunthorpe on Sunday afternoon, was held at Nottingham General Hospital this afternoon by Mr F.W. Rothera, the Deputy-City Coroner. The deceased, who was nearly 19 years of age, was the son of Mr C.H. Carryer, of Hampton House, Leicester. The Deputy Coroner explained at the outset that on Sunday the deceased, who was stationed in Warwickshire, left the depot intending to fly to Leicester. Apparently he got out of his bearings and descended near Gunthorpe. He appeared in starting again not to have risen sufficiently high to clear a building, with

the result that his machine struck it and fell to the ground. The petrol fired, and deceased received serious injuries. He was brought to the Nottingham General Hospital, where he died two hours later … The first witness was Second-Lieutenant Nigel Rupert Carryer, R.M., deceased's brother, who stated that deceased had intimated to him his intention to fly to Leicester on Sunday and alight in Western Park. Witness was there to meet him, and about five minutes to one an aeroplane passed over the park and disappeared in the clouds in the direction of Melton. About five o'clock witness was told his brother had had a mishap. He added that he had no complaint to make against anyone. His brother was flying on duty, and for his own convenience wished to descend at Leicester. He understood that the machine was the best in the squadron … Police Constable Cleal, of East Bridgford, said he saw an aeroplane passing over about 1.30 on Sunday. The aviator seemed to be in trouble, and witness thought he was coming down. He went to a spot near Trent side, and saw deceased, who asked to be directed to Leicester. The aviator then restarted his machine, and flew over the Trent very low – not more than 50 feet above the ground.

"I watched him for a couple of minutes," witness went on, "and all of a sudden he struck something. The next thing I saw was a cloud of smoke. He was then about 300 yards away. I got on my bicycle and cycled to the spot. I then found he had struck a loft at the top of a cowshed. The machine was lying on the ground in flames." Dr Duff, of East Bridgford, and Dr Brooks, of Lowdham, were sent for, and ordered the injured man's removal to the hospital. Witness added that when he spoke to deceased on the Trent side the latter said he was all right, but had lost his bearings. There was a strong wind blowing at the time. John Bradwell, of Gunthorpe, who was the first to arrive at the scene of the accident, said he found the airman on his hands and knees, he apparently having crawled several feet away from the machine. Witness spoke to him, asked him his name, but all he could say was, "Save me", several times. Another man came up, and he and witness carried the airman into the neighbouring field. Another eye-witness said that the propeller struck the top of the barn and went through the wall into the building. The injured man was brought to the hospital in Mr Gregory's car. He was semi-conscious, but could give no account of the accident. Captain Arthur Travers Harris [later known as 'Bomber' Harris], of the Royal Flying Corps, said he had known deceased since his learning to fly, and he always considered him a very good pilot. He had given him permission to use this particular machine, which was of a new type, when he liked. It was considered one of the safest types, and it had been tested the day before the accident. After questioning the police-constable, Captain Harris said it was quite obvious that Lieutenant Carryer lost control of the machine. What caused him to lose control he could not say. It was a very gusty day, and he considered it most likely that the airman was trying to turn when a gust of wind met the machine and "dipped" it to such an extent that he was unable to recover control before it hit the house. The jury returned a verdict of "Accidental death", and found that no blame attached to anyone. They expressed their sympathy with the relatives of the deceased.[14]

Late that summer of 1916, Jack Horner was given eight days leave to return home, before being posted to the reserve battalion of his

Leicester market place during the First World War

G 40648 LEICESTER: MARKET PLACE.

regiment. Horner had been wounded on the Somme with the 8th Leicesters, and had spent some weeks recovering in hospital in Plymouth. He was cheered by an experience which occurred when walking through Leicester; he called at a tailor's shop to have a wound stripe – a vertical brass strip about two inches long – sewn on to the cuff of his tunic, signifying that he had been injured in combat. The tailor, proud to be able to do something for the young soldier, would accept no money when Horner tried to pay for the work. However, another incident, which also occurred during that leave, was less gratifying. Horner tells us:

> I was in the Market Place, near the old shop of Simpkin and James – a man on a traditional soap box was telling the world at large that the troops and soldiers were made deliberately drunk, to force them to go into action. I listened with amazement, and I asked him if he had been in France, and in action. He said, "No".
>
> I asked him who had told him the story of soldiers being made drunk. He replied that it was common knowledge. I pressed him to say where he had all his information from. He could not give a reply.
>
> Then I let him have a few choice words, and told him he was a bloody liar (and I really meant that), and to keep his mouth shut, or I would shut it for him, as I had just been in the Battle of the Somme where I was wounded and sent to hospital, and was now on leave, and I told him (and by now a rather large crowd of people were listening to what I had to say), that if he thought that two jars of rum of one gallon each between seven or eight hundred men would make any man drunk, then I would pour the bloody lot down his throat.
>
> He got off his perch and walked off with a flea in his ear. Some of the people thanked me, including a policeman who had been listening to all that I told this man, and he told me that he had said the same thing about the troops and soldiers many times, and was very pleased indeed that I had put the teetotal fanatic in his place. He said he would keep an eye on him in future.[15]

The Market Place in September 1916 was also the venue for a unique

A group of men posing as women, probably appearing in a play as one of the entertainments at Leicester's Olde Englishe Faire in 1916. (Record Office)

fund raising venture organized by Mayor Jonathan North's £100,000 Committee. 'Ye Olde Englishe Faire' was a two-day event which aimed to raise £100,000 for disabled ex-servicemen in Leicester. All areas of society were involved, and more than fifty local firms contributed goods to be sold. As well as the market sale, there was entertainment throughout the event. These included Frolics concert party and Hamoril's pierrot troupe, performing in the Corn Exchange along with Mr Walter Groocock's Orchestra and New Military Band, the Band of the Leicestershire Regiment and the Band of Desford Industrial School. There were dozens of side shows, exhibitions and games and some nearby premises were thrown open to conducted tours. A correspondent of the *Leicester Daily Mercury*, describing the scene, reported:

> A large number of stalls were laden with fancy work and laces, dear to the hearts of the ladies while others were devoted to the severely utilitarian. What is there that one wanted? A fan, for your ladyfriend? Several dainty fans are exposed for sale. A shawl fit for a queen? You found the very thing, worn by the late Queen Victoria's mother, on Stall 50. Ornaments? Why, there are thousands of beautiful ornaments. Something for the office? There is the latest kind of typewriter on sale. You thought of the

children? Well there are dolls and toys galore. In fact one could, without leaving the Marketplace, pretty well furnish the home from top to bottom and at the same time, help a good cause. The gifts of the Elementary Schools children made a brave show and, naturally, attracted the parents. The Olde Chymist's Shoppe was well stocked, and trade was brisk, especially in toilet requisites. The smoker is not forgotten, for there is a stall where one can buy tobacco, cigars and cigarettes, pipes, etc. There are several well laden with sweets and chocolates, not forgetting the 'Leicester Rock'. On the stall presided over by the Mayoress, is to be found a great quantity of plain and fancy needlework, as

The cover of the souvenir booklet for Ye Olde Englishe Faire.

well as household linen and dainty underwear. The Belgian refugees have a stall on which the lace, for which that country is famous, is exhibited.[16]

Another fund-raising element was the tastefully printed and bound souvenir volume, locally produced by C.H. Gee & Co. It appeared as a limited edition and featured pictures of old Leicester, along with a text that extolled the bravery of the town's soldiers, sailors and airmen. In North's preface he stated:

Let it then be clearly understood that this [fund] is for Leicester lads, our neighbours, our shopmates, our employees, our own kith and kin, who went for that their Country's call and endured the horrors of war for the maintenance of our common rights. In due course some of those will return home incapable of again taking their place in the ordinary ranks of industry. To these we shall be unquestionably indebted, and it

Jonathan North, Mayor of Leicester during the Great War. The Faire was the brainchild of his £100,000 committee.

is unthinkable that we shall be unprepared when the time for the discharge of that obligation arrives. I wish further to say emphatically that there is no intention to use a single penny to relieve the State of its legitimate responsibility, but doubtless there will be cases where it will be both necessary and justifiable to supplement the Government pension. The main object, however, will be to provide new interests which will safeguard the men against the blighting and withering effects of a stagnant and aimless existence. It would be a national disaster if the war-disabled were left to themselves with nothing but war pensions. It is quite impossible, however, in this foreword to do more than fore-shadow what is desired to be accomplished. I can, therefore, only ask for the assent to the statement that time will surely reveal a need for such a fund. The details as regard to its general application will be dealt with later by a Committee to be appointed which will represent all local interests. Do what you can! Do all you can! You cannot do too much in return for the service and sacrifice of our Country's heroes, who went forth in their strength and now "weak and broken lie".[17]

CINEMA-DE-LUXE
GRANBY STREET, LEICESTER,
TO-DAY.

THE IDLER,
By C. HADDON-CHAMBERS

MONDAY NEXT and ALL THE WEEK,
Exclusive Pictures of

YE OLDE
ENGLISHE FAIRE,
SPECIALLY TAKEN FOR
AND
ONLY TO BE SEEN AT THE

CINEMA - DE - LUXE.
COME AND SEE YOURSELF ON
THE SCREEN.
Your one and only chance to see
this film.
ALSO,
MONDAY, TUESDAY & WEDNESDAY

CHARLES CHAPLIN
In his Great Comedy

EASY MONEY.
Also, a Five Act Triangle Drama,

BETWEEN MEN.
A HUGE AND BRILLIANT
PROGRAMME.

A newspaper advertisement for a film of the Olde Englishe Faire. Locally shot newsreels were a feature of this era; sadly, most are now lost.

The souvenir booklet closed with a nominal roll of the women of Leicester who had helped to run the stalls during the event, numbering some 430 names – another impressive testament to the scale to which the female population put their shoulder to the wheel not just in industry and nursing but in fundraising also.

That autumn, Sapper Dougherty was also back in Leicester on leave, and one evening whilst walking his sweetheart home he heard the sound of a factory hooter indicating that a Zeppelin raid was expected. The German airships had sufficient range from their bases on the North Sea coast to reach the Midlands, and considerable destruction had been caused in raids elsewhere. Dougherty, however, had already encountered them in France. He continues:

A lady shopkeeper recommended us to lie down, as her son at the front had told her, but I knew there was no immediate danger or I should have heard the engines which made quite a noise. She meant well...[18]

Dougherty found the false alarm amusing but to others they were more dramatic. Betty Preston was a child during the war and recalled:

I can remember the Zeppelins coming over ... It was exciting to us, because we were children ... We saw these long things in the sky, I remember one night ever so plainly, and ever so many of us were in Checketts Road looking at these, and we could see these long cigar shaped things, and the searchlight on them.[19]

Unlike Loughborough, Leicester was never bombed during the First World War, but elaborate air raid precautions were put in place, with real concerns that the Germans would extend the chemical warfare which they had introduced on the Western Front to the civilian populations as well. Chief Constable H. Allen issued an Air Raids warning notice, part of which stated that in the event of a raid:

The public are strongly advised to remain at home. The windows and doors of the lower floors should be closed to prevent the admission of noxious gases in case of poisonous bombs being dropped etc. A supply of water or wet sand should be kept ready so that a small fire could be promptly and effectively dealt with.[20]

For young children the threat of Zeppelins was perhaps the most compelling aspect of the war, which often seemed distant and unreal. Another Leicester youngster, Margot Cliff remembered:

I never remember being frightened by the war. It was just a fact of life - except when I saw an airship and assumed it was a

Leicester sisters Margot (right) and Gwen Cliff, during the First World War.
(Courtesy of Gillian Lighton)

Zeppelin. I was frightened by pictures of the Irish troubles though. Ireland seemed at home, Flanders somewhere else.[21]

Margot began her school career around this time. She recalled:

I started Medway Street School in September 1916. Actually the school was 'evacuated' to Melbourne Road because Medway Street premises were used as a clearing station for the war wounded as it lay between the station and the City General. There were many war wounded in the area, all in hospital-blue uniform. We went to school half time - mornings one week and afternoons the other, afternoons being long then until 5pm. So we always had three hours schooling. There was a homework system but it hardly applied to young infants. I remember once taking the word 'me' home on a pink card to learn to spell it, read it, or something ....I remember going into the 'babies class' until I turned 5 in October. I sat with a smartly dressed little boy who had wavy dark hair and brown eyes. He wore a brown tunic with a cream broderie anglaise collar over his shorts. All I remember about that class was in the afternoons we had to put our heads on our arms on the desk and go to sleep! Shades of the beginnings of nursery classes.

Classrooms all had dual desks. The writing surface lifted up and I remember once chalking something on the underside. There was a shelf underneath where we put our lunch. I never understood why we needed to eat between breakfast and dinner, but we always took something. I don't know what it normally was but bread dipped in bacon fat was popular. The desks were of course arranged in serried ranks with the teacher's desk on a platform at the front, with a cupboard on the side wall and a swing blackboard or blackboard and easel.[22]

As the 1916/17 Association Football season got underway that autumn, the call-up of the cream of Britain's youth had made itself felt among the players, though clubs were beginning to come to terms with the vagaries of wartime football. With regular first team players away on war service, but players from other teams sometimes posted to the district or available on a one-off basis, a 'guest player' system flourished. Leicester Fosse would call upon no less than seventy-two guest players during the course of this season alone. Fielding a full team was often a challenge, and the home game against Grimsby Town that September was not the only match which Fosse would start with a ten man side. Fortunately on this occasion, after a quarter of an hour, former 'Fossil' Albert Trueman was spotted in the stand, and was persuaded to take to the pitch!

On 28 October, against Lincoln City at Filbert Street, another former Fosse favourite made his final appearance for the club, this time as a guest player. Leicester-born Tommy Benfield had been one of the biggest stars of the Leicester side prior to the war. In an away match he had scored the first ever goal at Arsenal's new Highbury ground, before he was sold to Derby for a then record sum to try to ease the financial difficulties which Fosse were in. In 1914, like so many professional footballers, he had joined the army, and a brief spell of leave must have found him at home and available for duty with his old club that day. Sadly, he would never return to football, being killed in action in the final months of the war, serving with the Leicestershire Regiment.

At Christmas 1916, Leicester engineering firm Jones & Shipman produced a small souvenir booklet to accompany the parcel of Christmas gifts which the firm sent to each of its former employees at the front. The booklet contained a number of letters to the men from senior figures in the company, which as well as news from home, expressed their appreciation of the sacrifices made by the fighting men. One, from the Patriotic and Benevolent Fund Committee, gave an indication that the wartime workforce was now from a broader cross-section of society than that of pre-war days, even if the women which the firm had taken on to cope with increased war production were mentioned as something of an afterthought:

Leicester footballer Tommy Benfield. The former Fosse player made a brief final appearance at Filbert Street in 1916; he was killed in action in France in 1918.

> Considerable changes have taken place since your departure. The firm has progressed and enlarged its borders, and now provides employment for more than twice the number of those who worked here at the outbreak of war. But despite these changes, men and boys, old hands and new starters – aye and the girls as well all unite to remember you this Christmastide, and in the name of all we have to offer you our sincere wishes for the best that is possible to you under existing circumstances, with the hope that your efforts will help to win through to a great success which will bring this war to an early end.[23]

Female munitions workers in Leicester in 1916.

The chairman of the company, Frank Shipman, meanwhile added a personal message:

> The country has need of each one of you now wearing His Majesty's uniform, as it has need of every one of us now employed in meeting the requirements of the many National Workshops and Munition Factories.
>
> As we in the works remember the great efforts and sacrifices that you are making, may we be more firmly resolved to do "our little bit" to the utmost of our ability.
>
> I cannot let this opportunity pass without assuring each one of you of my own interest, and indeed that of every one with whom you worked, in your own personal welfare, and of my pleasure to be associated with the parcel which is being sent to you as a small token of the regard and esteem which we bear towards you.[24]

Lastly, a letter from Frederick R.Cates, the company secretary, expressed a clear understanding of what the men at the front were enduring:

> Comrades, we do not forget you, though you may not very often hear from us, for we are a pretty busy crowd nowadays and could very well do with your help again, yet we often wish we heard more of you and knew more of your daily doings which we imagine to be so much more exciting than the dull routine of our business life.
>
> We sympathize with you in your hardships while you rough it through the winter, extracting, as an Englishman does, what pleasure you can, for we know that through the muddy drudgery of it all you are working and fighting in the most just cause for which war has ever been waged and that it is by your efforts that we at home are enabled to live and work in peace and comfort.[25]

Mountings for naval guns being produced at the British United Shoe Machinery works on Belgrave Road, 1916.

Shells in the paintshop at Belgrave Gate, ready for dispatch to the filling plants.

If Britain were to be successful in this momentous life or death struggle in which she now found herself, then there could be no clearer expression or acknowledgement of the fact that those on the home front and those on the fighting fronts were as vital as each other. Indeed, the two were mutually interdependent; yet the coming year would strain both of these pillars of the British war effort almost to breaking point.

CHAPTER 4

Great unrest

In spite of the growing awareness that the outcome of the war was going to be decided in the factories of Britain as much as it would be on the battlefields of France, the year of 1917 would prove to be one particularly characterized by industrial unrest and disputes, on a scale scarcely seen before in the history of British labour relations. Militarily, it would also be a frustrating and disappointing year, as the allies tried repeatedly to break the deadlock on the Western Front; in spite of enormous casualties, by the year's end the Germans appeared to be as firmly entrenched on French and Belgian soil as they had ever been.

In Leicester, in February 1917 the question of who would have overall command of the town's Volunteers was finally resolved when Colonel J.E. Sarson agreed to step into the breach. One of Leicester's longest serving amateur soldiers, Sarson had in fact commanded a previous battalion of Volunteers in the years leading up to the Boer War, and he was widely respected in military cicles within the town. Sarson applied himself to the vexed questions which were troubling the Leicester Volunteers at this time, one of which was the fact that the battalion had become so large, swelled as it was by exempted men, that it was now quite unwieldy. It would take Sarson several months, however, to obtain

Colonel J.E. Sarson, who in February 1917 took over command of the Leicester Volunteers.

permission from the War Office to split it into two. Difficulties continued in other areas, as the officers had little scope for redress in cases where men absented themselves from training or other duties. In many instances the men had legitimate reasons for being absent, as either their other duties as Special Constables took precedence, or they were required for extra hours in the munitions works in which they were employed.

The same month, what was seen as the continuing erosion of the moral fabric of society in Leicester was challenged by the congregation of Melbourne Hall Evangelical Free Church. Its historian Ernest E. Kendall recorded that:

> The cinema had now become one of the main attractions of the times, and when permission to open on Sunday was given *ostensibly for the benefit of the troops* stationed in and around Leicester, the congregation on Sunday evening, February 18th, 1917, by a standing vote, passed a strongly worded resolution, deprecating the encroachment on the sanctity of the Sabbath. Copies were sent to the Mayor, the Watch Committee and the local press.[1]

Kendall observed ruefully that this was a wartime measure which had since become an established practice; in common with so many changes brought about by the exigencies of the First World War, once the tightly bound moral constraints of Victorian England were loosened it was found to be impossible to put the genie back in the bottle. The Melbourne Hall congregation were, however, concerned not only with the cinema but also with that old chestnut, alcohol. Kendall continues:

> At the same evening service, there was passed a resolution respectfully and earnestly appealing to the Prime Minister to take immediate steps to prohibit the drink traffic "during the war and period of demobilisation" … In spite of the king's example to abstain for the period of the war, and of Lord Kitchener's appeal to the public through the press, not to 'treat' the lads who were doing their best to fit themselves for service, there was a sad amount of drunkenness. Strong evidence for some restriction was presented to Leicester Licensing Authority by an influential

deputation and the magistrates decided to curtail the hours of sale – *by thirty minutes*! Prior to a town plebiscite, a faithful band captained by Arthur Thornton, canvassed the district allocated to Melbourne Hall, but the final result was a majority of 1,253 (of those who voted) against prohibition during the war and demobilization.[2]

Once again the temperance movement had found itself in the minority among the people of Leicester. Overall however, churches performed an important function during the war in offering moral support – indeed mutual support – to communities undergoing severe emotional stress, with many of their young men at the front. The lovingly tended rolls of honour to be found in most churches testified to their central place at the heart of the communities which they served. Many went further by providing direct aid to the soldiers from their congregations. Edith Isaac's husband George, a private in the 7th Battalion Leicestershire Regiment, was a prisoner of war. Edith remembered many years later the shock and anxiety caused by the news that her husband was missing, but her local church near the couple's home on New Road in Leicester was able to help with practical matters:

> …we had a vicar … there and they were interested with the prisoners of war and they used to pay him ten shillings a month and he used to keep the boys in shoes and food, parcels you know, and because we couldn't send them so he used to and my husband said that it kept him alive, the food as they sent…. [3]

The pressures of war had by this stage begun to make themselves felt even in that temple of learning, the Museum and Art Gallery on New Walk in Leicester. As early as March 1915 fuel-saving lighting restrictions had forced it to end its evening openings, and now new exhibitions were focused mainly on various aspects of the war effort, such as 'food saving'. This became even more important as imports were seriously affected by German U-boat attacks on merchant shipping, and a 'Food Economy' exhibition which opened at the Museum in May 1917 attracted over 100,000 visitors. The Museums and Libraries Committee was subsequently asked by the Ministry of Food to release its Curator, Dr E.E. Lowe, for three months to take

Two 'Roll of Honour' cards from Hinckley Road Primitive Methodist Church. The churches were focal points for community pride in the part their sons were playing in the war. Almost every church had a roll of honour of some sort.

'general oversight of Food Economy Exhibitions' on a national basis. Though reluctant, it felt it must comply – but only on condition that any extra expense incurred due to his absence would be repaid by the Ministry.

It was becoming clearer by the day that only if every aspect of British society were mobilized toward the war effort could victory be achieved. The voracious appetite of the army on the Western Front demanded more and more output from industry. Pochin tells us:

Private William Henry Cox, 6th Leicesters. Killed on 11 April 1917, he was formerly a conductor on the Leicester Corporation Tramways.

For the prosecution of the war, iron and steel production was pressed harder and harder with consequent pressure on ironstone and limestone output. Cement production rose under similar circumstances. This and the shortage of manpower brought into being the greater application of mechanical means for digging and handling the vast quantities of raw material required. The company [Goodwin Barsby] designed and built several large machines for this

purpose. Each had a large screen or rumbler, mounted on rollers, paths and trunnions for separating the material into sizes for getting rid of the dirt and smalls. Each machine was also equipped with boom conveyors for stacking and loading purposes, and the whole mounted on wheels to run on rail tracks alongside the mechanical shovels. One of these machines was so large that the works gates

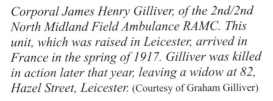

Corporal James Henry Gilliver, of the 2nd/2nd North Midland Field Ambulance RAMC. This unit, which was raised in Leicester, arrived in France in the spring of 1917. Gilliver was killed in action later that year, leaving a widow at 82, Hazel Street, Leicester. (Courtesy of Graham Gilliver)

had to be taken down to get it out. It was drawn to the railway station by a steam tractor engine and along one of the city streets, the authorities were so fearful of the sewers and water mains, that a timber track was laid before it, as it progressed … In 1917, the War Office also gave the company a development contract for a combined trench-digger, cable layer and back-filling machine. It was covered by the patent of G.A. Chapman, a local engineer who supervised its construction. No machine of this type had been made in this country before and a great deal of experimental work was carried out.[4]

Not everyone in industry, however, was pulling in the same direction. In May 1917 came the three-week long Engineers' Strike, one of the most serious cases of industrial unrest in the war so far. Also called the Shop Stewards' Strike, it came about as a result of the flood of unskilled workers – male and female – into the industry resulting from the Munitions of War Act. The shop stewards were emboldened by events in Russia where the February 1917 revolution briefly promised a workers' democracy, and the strike was a protest by shop floor activists as much against their own union hierarchies (which had disavowed it) as against the government. Leicester was among the places worst affected by the dispute, and the government posted notices in such areas reminding the strikers that the stoppage of work by engineers engaged in the manufacture of munitions had occurred at a moment when, in view of the offensives taking place on all fronts, there was a greater need for shells than at any previous time. The *Leicester Mercury* took a dim view of the matter, and reported in an editorial that:

It is decidedly disquieting to read as we do today that the strikes of engineers in various parts of the country are not only continuing but increasing. There is reason for profound regret that anything of the kind should have been possible at such a juncture as the present, either through delay in the adjustment of grievances or by reason of the haste with which the strikers have put their own adjustable complaints before the overwhelming national interest, with which is bound up the lives of our men at the front. One wonders if those who stop work on essential supplies for the army realise what they are doing. If they do realise, and still stop work then they at least ought to see that by doing so they are playing the enemy game insidiously and effectively.[5]

The newspaper also printed stories of strikers being taunted by munition girls as shirkers and cowards, using their exempted status to avoid military service, alongside reports of a wounded soldier home on leave flooring two striking engineers with a blow each to the jaw, but the stories were strangely lacking in detail and had more than a whiff of propaganda (at which the British Government was so adept) about them. Having tried and failed to negotiate with the strikers, the government invoked the Defence of the Realm Act and arrested the strike leaders, who were taken to London and arraigned at the Bow Street Magistrates Court. Ultimately they were released, but the implication was that the government would not be so lenient next time. Among those who appeared in court was the leader of the dispute in Leicester, Dave Ramsay.

Ramsay was a pattern maker by trade, a member of the Amalgamated Society of Engineers, and later of the Amalgamated Engineering Union; he was also a member of the Socialist Labour Party in Leicester. An anti-war activist, he had the previous year been fined £100 for attempting to prejudice recruiting to the army. Ramsay was part of the inner circle of activists involved in building 'workers' committees' across Britain, in the model of the Clyde Workers' Committee. Declaring himself a committed Bolshevik, in November 1918 he was described in British police files as 'advocating revolution with machine guns' at a meeting that included Sylvia Pankhurst as a speaker. A speech given to a large Daily Herald League rally in a Croydon cinema eventually led to his conviction and imprisonment for sedition.

Dave Ramsay, Leicester shop steward of the Amalgamated Society of Engineers. He led the Leicester branch in the 1917 engineering strike, and was one of the ring leaders arrested by the government under the Defence of the Realm Act.
(Courtesy of Graham Stevenson)

The ongoing discontent in the factories was not the only source of division in British society in

1917. The running sore of conscription and the bitterness which it provoked, had not gone away. Another trade unionist, Rowland Hill, had been active in the Labour movement since 1905, and was President of the Leicester branch of the National Union of Clerks from 1909. By 1914 he was president of the Trades Council, and by 1917 active both within the ILP and the Union of Democratic Control in the town. He made no secret of his anti-war credentials, and was actually sent a white feather through the post, accompanied by an abusive message. That year he was called up into the army, but claimed exemption from military service as a conscientious objector. The local tribunal granted him a deferment of service only, and when this expired he went on the run, effectively as a deserter from the army. In spite of this, he continued to write for the left wing *Leicester Pioneer* newspaper under the pen name of Robert Dale.

Rowland Hill, a member of the Union of Democratic Control and a conscientious objector. When an application for exemption from military service was refused, he went on the run as a deserter. (Courtesy of Ned Newitt)

Strikers and the so-called 'conchies' inspired equal revulsion among the front-line troops, and some idea of the opinion of most Leicester soldiers towards the COs can be gained from the writing of Dick Read. He remembered a spell in the summer of 1917 spent at the Leicestershire Regiment depot at Wigston, where he encountered a squad of conscientious objectors from Leicester and the county being drilled by a colour sergeant:

> I looked, and saw them slouching slowly round the perimeter of the barrack square, with the sergeant and the escort of two men keeping up with them, as they deliberately flouted authority by studied insolence and nonchalance amounting to open defiance. If hate is the word, I hated these figures of men just then, far more than any German. At least the Germans were worthy of respect as fighters, but when I thought of what my mates might possibly be enduring then, in front of Fontaine les Croisilles, while these long-haired apologies for men skulked at home and went to these extremes to avoid what we deemed to be their clear responsibilities to their country … Almost fifty years later, I'm

afraid I still feel the same about 99 per cent of them and their kind … During the six weeks or so that I was at the depot, my duties brought me into contact with a good many of them. I met only one who, in my opinion and that of my colleagues there, genuinely objected to military service on religious grounds…[6]

Sometimes around this time, Read was detailed to carry out duties which involved firing a volley over the grave of comrades who had succumbed to battlefield injuries in hospitals in England. He remembered:

Sergeant Dick Read, who commanded the firing party at a number of local funerals.

…I was NCO in charge of the firing party at more than a dozen military funerals, mostly of soldiers dying of wounds at the great base hospital in Leicester, the actual interments taking place at the nearby Welford Road Cemetery. Several times a week, midday saw me parading my party, generally unchanged, running through the reversed arms drill and volley firing before the break for dinner. Then parade again, this time ready to march off. A quick check of uniforms, buttons, boots and webbing, followed by rifle inspection and the issue of three blank cartridges per man (the spent cases of which had to be picked up from the grave side and returned to store) and off we went to the nearby village station where we took the train for Leicester … the buglers and one man carrying a large folded Union Flag bringing up the rear.

We became quite expert at this job; that is to say, conversant with the various burial services, and, with a little practice, able to get the necessary orders executed smartly and volleys which rang out like a single shot, instead of a ragged imitation of a *feu de joie*. Indeed, until I had mastered the necessary technique, I was always on thorns until the ceremony was over, particularly when a crowd was present, which was frequently the case…

A crowd gathers to watch the military funeral of a Leicester soldier.

Somehow, however all this business seemed so unnecessary to us in the light of what we had seen in France, that we made grim jokes about it all in carrying out our parts of the ceremonial. To us it was a form of showmanship, a convention, possibly to satisfy the mourners, but we asked ourselves repeatedly what possible good it did – as though the poor, torn and frequently gangrened soldier within the coffin, to whom the last call had come at length as a merciful release from pain, knew anything about it![7]

Read's mention of Fontaine les Croisilles was a reference to a bitter battle fought earlier that spring by the Leicestershire battalions of Kitchener's Army. In an effort to break through the Hindenburg Line, the four battalions had hurled themselves at carefully prepared belts of barbed wire, guarded by well sited machine-guns. The result had been an ignominious failure, with many members of the 8th and 9th Leicesters – who had penetrated some distance into the Hindenburg Line before being cut off – captured by the enemy. A Leicester soldier, Arthur Cave, recorded his impressions of the attack in his diary for 3 May 1917. Cave was before the war a clerk in the Hart and Levy hosiery factory, and now held the rank of Regimental Quartermaster

Sergeant in the 7th Leicesters, a remarkable achievement for a young man of just 24 years of age. He wrote:

> Battle of Bullecourt, our grand failure. The 8th and 9th attacked the Hindenburg Line, with the 6th and 7th in reserve. After the attacking battalions had captured Fontaine Wood and Cherisy they had to retire, the 7th Battalion attacking to cover their withdrawal. The attack was carried out in complete darkness, and the enemy seemed to be well aware of our intentions. A heavy barrage came down simultaneously with our own and owing to darkness units rapidly lost touch with those on their flanks. Over a thousand yards of no man's land had to be covered before the enemy was reached.[8]

Arthur Cave, seen shortly before enlistment into the 7th Leicesters. He lived at 24 Melbourne Street.
(Courtesy of Colonel Terry Cave)

News of missing loved ones was slow to trickle through to those on the home front, and out of desperation the parents of those who were not accounted for sought information from the families of local officers. Two such letters were received that summer by the father of one Leicesters' officer, Canon F.B. Pitts. That from Mrs Emma Hancox Soden, of 69 Hawkesbury Road, Leicester, read:

> I can assure you Sir there is getting a great unrest amongst the people its just on the balance of a revolt it's the cruel way in which our boys are treated when prisoners. There's plenty of money being collected and we feel something ought to be done to get us news of our boys in Germany they have committed no crime but we give them willingly for the country but this cruelty we cannot bear. Something will have to be done I am no revolutionary only a quiet woman of 67 but cannot help hearing the murmur amongst the people we only want justice for the boys and may God in his mercy protect them all.[9]

From 61 Merridale Road, Leicester came a similar letter from a Mrs Tutty, who wrote:

> I hope you will excuse me writing to you but I saw in the paper that your son is a prisoner of war in Germany and my son has been missing ever since the 9th of May and he was my son's officer wich [sic] he was servant to and i [sic] have not heard any thing of him only that he was reported missing and I am a widow mother and I am anxious to know tidings of him Sir would you be kind enough to wright [sic] and ask your son if he knew anything about him as I shall be pleased to know.[10]

Sadly both Privates Hancox and Tutty had been killed in action, and their bodies were never identified, prolonging the agony of their loved ones. The grief of Leicester and her people caused by the terrible human cost of this war was focused that summer upon a temporary war memorial, erected in the Town Hall Square and unveiled on 28 June 1917 by Henry John Manners. Designed by S. Perkins Pick and Benjamin John Fletcher, the war memorial was constructed by Joseph Herbert Morcom with lettering made by masters and students of Leicester School of Art. The memorial was made from brick, cement and plaster with sculptural relief designs which included a pelican bleeding itself to feed its young; although it was not intended to be a permanent structure, it remained in place until the 1950s.

1917 would not be a successful year for the western allies on the battlefield. The lack of progress at Arras and the Hindenburg Line in the spring would be followed by bitter fighting around Ypres in the late summer and autumn. The Third Battle of Ypres (popularly known as Passchendaele) is etched into the British folk memory as one of the bitterest battles of the First World War. It was fought in a flooded, desolate landscape of waterlogged shell holes, in which every tree

Florence Egerton, a VAD at the 5th Northern General Hospital in Leicester.
(Courtesy of the University of Leeds)

In Memory of Leicester's Fallen Heroes,
1914 - 1917.

The temporary memorial erected in the Town Hall Square in June 1917. It was pulled down in the 1950s, in what was described as an act of civic vandalism.

and house had been destroyed by a systematic and relentless bombardment. The battle was also characterized by heavy use of poison gas, which contaminated the water in the shell holes and caused more casualties, in particular deadly mustard gas, introduced by the Germans. It burned eyes, skin, and lungs if inhaled, and the suffering of those who came into contact with it was appalling. In August the first casualties of the battle began to reach Leicester. Florence Egerton was a member of the Voluntary Aid Detachment, assisting nurses at the 5th Northern General Hospital. She was a young woman as dedicated to her cause as it was possible to find and although she was not a trained nurse, this was clearly her vocation. In one letter she wrote to her mother:

> …on Wednesday a convoy came in and we had 15 of the worst cases I have ever seen. Its selfish of me to describe them but I want you to realize what the work is that calls and grips me. One boy of 20 has two fractured legs with gaping wounds and has to be drugged till he's simple and is practically helpless. It takes 3 of us to make his bed. Another has a gash from the mouth, along the jaw (fractured) down the neck and on to [the] shoulder. It is

sewn up as far as the jaw and then, all the length of the jaw is an open, dirty gash. It's the most gruesome thing I've seen. He also has a wound in one arm, on his ankle and his thigh and is as patient as a lamb. He never gets cross even over feeding which is just awful. Another has a shrapnel wound in [the] thigh and has also been gassed with the <u>new</u> gas. Its hellish – his body is literally scorched nearly black all over, while some parts eg legs and arms, face and neck are a mass of blisters as from burns. His eyes are made up and his voice nearly gone. Yet he still smiles. Those are the worst, but the others each have more than one wound. In all, we have 24 patients for dressings in a morning – a few at night according to how they feel, and 27 beds backs and washings of helpless patients in an evening. Add to this the fact that until today we have had no nurse and you will know why my off duty time has generally been afternoon when I've rested mostly … its just a bare fact that from somewhere I have got one gift to be thankful for – nursing … I can only use [it] for a short time while the war lasts and really I feel as if I must.[11]

The battle for Passchendaele again involved the four Leicestershire battalions of the 110th Brigade as well as the 1st Leicesters and the 11th Battalion (Midland Pioneers). Jack Horner was present with the 6th Battalion, Leicestershire Regiment. His battalion was moving forward to support an attack when they came under German shellfire. Horner wrote later:

My company, 'A' were moving up in single file in support of the 9th Battalion, when from nowhere (I don't remember hearing or seeing any shelling) a piece of shrapnel hit my left forearm. I was knocked flat, and when I came round I was alone with a smashed arm. I gripped my arm above the elbow with my right hand to stop the blood flow, and somehow got my arm lying across my stomach, the blood soaking my tunic.[12]

Identity discs of Private Albert Finney, of Leicester, who died of wounds in October 1917. The discs would have been returned to his next of kin with his personal effects.

With no stretcher bearers in sight, Horner had no choice but to try to make his own way to the rear:

> I stumbled on, God knows where, for I don't – through the mud and slime, on this great sea of mud. I didn't know where I was going, or how long I had been stumbling around, for I saw no one, and in all this space, no one saw me. Honestly, I have no recollection whatever of these wanderings. It was dusk, maybe night time, when I saw a chink of light some distance away, and I made for it as best I could.
>
> It was a German Pill Box. I went in, and again almost faded out, but, Thank Heaven! They were British, using the Pill Box as an advanced Dressing Station, by stretcher bearers and medical orderlies. I asked for water (I can still taste the petrol in that water now). They asked me where the Hell I'd come from. I couldn't tell them, I was all in, but they knew from my shoulder flashes which division I came from, and that was …miles away.[13]

Captain Charles Eaton, 11th Leicesters. He died of wounds on 9 August 1917, during the Third Battle of Ypres. His mother lived at 24 Evington Drive, Leicester.

As the offensive continued through the late summer and autumn of 1917, the pain of bereavement would be felt in more and more Leicester homes, as the price of pressing home the offensive was felt in a steadily growing casualty list. We have a poignant insight into what this pain meant to one Leicester mother, whose son Ernie Gays was killed in action near Ypres in September 1917, whilst serving with the Army Cyclist Corps. She wrote to one of Ernie's comrades, who had sent his condolences:

> 44, Milligan Road,
> Leicester. Sunday, 9 September 1917
>
> Dear friend,
> I am addressing you as a friend as any friend of my boy's is my friend. I thank you for sending us word of how our dear Ernest died. We also had a very nice letter from the Captain (Capt. E.

Johnston) the day before we received yours. It is a dreadful thought to lose our dear boy in this way. We would not believe it until we had a letter from someone who saw him. Did you see my boy after he died, could you tell us how he was? I should like to know what time of the day or night it happened (or thereabouts). Was he up the doings (are you allowed to tell us?) or was he on Sentry? I am sure we are all the while thinking of you dear lads, hoping and praying for you to be kept safe, and then when these awful tidings are sent us it shakes our faith. But then again when we get calm we know that God is still in heaven and He orders all things for the best.

I sent Ernie a parcel off on 21 August; if you should see anything of it, will you share what is good between you and his friends. I will never forget you and hope that you will write often to me.

So thanking you I close.

Yours truly, Mrs.Gays
P.S. Write soon.[14]

In industry however, the pressure of war, in particular the rising cost of living, began to make itself felt in the increasing number of disputes. Across Britain as a whole 5.5 million working days were lost to strikes in 1917, about double the figure for the previous year. The Government money which was pouring into engineering and munitions factories, together with the manpower shortage created by the war, and the conciliatory attitude of the Ministry of Munitions, which was desperate to keep workers at their lathes, encouraged union militancy. Shop stewards saw this as moment as a golden opportunity; for years industrial workers had suffered the ravages of capitalism and now the boot was on the other foot. Leicester was no exception to this rule. A cabinet report prepared by the Ministry of Labour summarized the situation for the week ending 3 October 1917 thus:

Kingsley S. Gimson, managing director of Gimson's Ironworks on Vulcan Road. He oversaw the firm's production of armaments, in co-operation with other Leicester engineering works.

The Vulcan Foundry. A large new factory, the Vulcan works was built for Gimson's near Humberstone Road between 1876 and 1879. Josiah Gimson was quickly established as an important and influential manufacturer in Leicester. His engineering firm was one of the largest in the city and prided itself on being a model employer in terms of wages and conditions of work.

At Leicester about 120 Engineers have been idle during the past week at Messrs Mellor, Bromley & Co's works. The trouble arose owing to the dismissal of a man who had refused to complete certain work which had been commenced by a Belgian, in receipt of a considerably higher rate of pay, unless he were paid the same rate. A meeting of the Leicester Iron Trades Federation took place on September 26th and it was resolved to notify the Ministry of Munitions that unless negotiations were instituted at once a general strike of members of the Federation would take place. An investigation is now taking place and the men returned to work on Monday last.

This strike has attracted considerable attention locally as has also that of the garment workers at Messrs Hart & Levy (Leicester) which has now been in progress some weeks. Over 800 employees are affected, the remaining 1,000 being still at work. The point in dispute is whether a bonus granted for army work should not be extended to civil work. The firm refuse to make any concession but are prepared to take the strikers back on the old conditions, meanwhile they are introducing new workpeople.[15]

It should not, however, be assumed that all of Leicester's Trade Unionists were from the anti-war camp. Unlike the majority of his colleagues in the ILP, Freddy Richards of the Boot and Shoe union supported the war. He recalled:

I advised both my boys to join up and should have done so myself if I had thought that by doing so I could have done more good. I have sung the 'Red Flag' and was prepared to fight for it and kill militarism in this or any other land.[16]

Freddy Richards of the Boot and Shoe Workers' Union. Unlike many others on the political left and in the trade union movement, he supported the war.
(Courtesy of Ned Newitt)

It is not known for sure why, in 1917, he declined the award of a CBE for his services to the war effort, but perhaps it was a gesture towards his anti-war colleagues, with whom he was becoming increasingly unpopular. Certainly in August 1918, this pro-war stance was the reported reason for his rejection as the Labour parliamentary candidate for Northampton.

In spite of the war being in its fourth year now, there was still a lively entertainment scene in Leicester in December 1917. In one week in that month the Palace Theatre featured Whit Cunliffe, the popular comedian. The *Leicester Mercury* described his cheery songs such as 'No Complaints' and 'Carry On' as raising hearty laughter from the audience, whilst his optimism was infectious. Also on the bill were Beatie and Babs, two comediennes who performed amusing songs and dances in *Kitchen Follies* whilst Woodward and Page completed the bill. The Pavilion meanwhile boasted a revue entitled *Life and Laughter* featuring the eight Brewster girls. Other prominent artistes in the show were Charles Eaton and Harry Bent. For those interested in the latest form of entertainment, the Picture House on Granby Street was screening the cinematic version of John Galsworthy's novel *Justice*. In the film, the leading character, played by Gerald du Maurier, resolves

Members of the Leicester Women's Volunteer Reserve, who in late 1916 and 1917 volunteered as part of their duties to whitewash kerbstones, protruding steps and other obstacles to pedestrians during wartime restrictions on street lighting.

to save Ruth Honeywell (played by Hilda Moore) from the hands of a brutal husband, but his efforts lead to his own imprisonment. The Floral Hall, meanwhile, was showing an American film entitled *A Gamble in Souls* starring Dorothy Dalton and William Desmond as an actress and a missionary cast adrift together on a desert island. Also on the bill was *Dorothy Dares*, another American picture starring and directed by Ruth Stonehouse.

For Leicester conscientious objector Horace Twilley, Christmas that year would be spent incarcerated in Wormwood Scrubs prison. The day passed easier for Twilley, however, thanks to the sound of carols which drifted over the high walls to him. He would have been cheered by the knowledge that these were not merely passing wassailers, but were in fact the choir of the Leicester No-Conscription Fellowship, who had come faithfully to sing hymns to him every Sunday since April of that year. Leicester had one of the longest established NCF choirs in the country, and one of its members wrote to other branches, advising them to set up similar ensembles and to make use of them outside prisons where their members were held:

> Providing one is able to stand within hearing distance of the ugly walls, it does not take many voices to send a 'volley' of music 'over the top'.[17]

The tactic was both of value in supporting the morale of imprisoned COs, and also made a useful propaganda tool. However, the coming year of 1918, as well as witnessing the end game in the long drawn out struggle in France between the Allies and the Germans, would also see the conclusion of the increasingly bitter game of cat and mouse being conducted at home between the pacifists and anti-conscription activists and the British Government.

CHAPTER 5

Vindicated before the world

By the end of 1917 the U-boat campaign against Allied shipping had almost succeeded in bringing Britain to her knees. In the final months of that year food reserves had run perilously low, and 1918 opened with the introduction of rationing on dairy products and meat. Initially, food control had been voluntary and it was introduced locally rather than nationally in a somewhat ad hoc fashion. Five months earlier, Leicester borough council had appointed a Food Control Committee, which first concerned itself with the distribution of sugar and some 60,000 sugar ration cards were issued to Leicester families. Butter rationing began in Leicester, the first place in Britain to introduce it, on 7 January 1918, with each person allowed four ounces per week of either butter or margarine. By February, beef, mutton and pork were also rationed, and the amount available to each individual was reduced as the food crisis deepened. In addition, meatless days in hotels and restaurants were introduced.

That month, Leicester members of the various railway unions met at the Bond Street Club to discuss the situation; the railwaymen had seen the ample supplies available in dining cars on trains, whilst the railway draymen had seen food supplies piled up at the rear of grocers' premises whilst queues formed at the front. The railwaymen believed that official incompetence rather than shortage was responsible for much of the inadequacy in food supply, and whilst they accepted that

Corporal Thomas Burden, Machine Gun Corps, formerly a shoe hand of Shakespeare Street, Leicester. He was wounded near Jerusalem and died of wounds in hospital in Egypt in January 1918.

there must be some hardship, which had to be endured, they believed that it should be borne fairly. A motion was moved – and accepted – that:

> ... this conference, viewing with alarm the food shortage arising as the result of muddle and unequal distribution of supplies demands that the Government shall immediately ration the whole of the people with the supplies now available. We advise branches to stop work on Saturday of each week as a protest against the inactivity of the Government, and the scandalous conditions whereby our womenfolk have to stand in queues for hours to obtain food which they could not otherwise get owing to inadequate distribution arrangements. We are of the opinion that this is likely to have very serious after effects on the health of our wives and children and therefore recommend that the men should use the day off to take their places in the queues, and by so doing assist to bring this disgraceful state of affairs to an end.[1]

Burden's grave in Hadra War Cemetery, Alexandria, photographed in late 1918.

The same week, Leicester pork butchers met to discuss what could be done to alleviate the queues outside their shops. The same newspaper reported that:

> At the request of the Food Control Committee it was agreed to open to the public on two mornings of the week, viz on Tuesdays and Fridays at 6.30am to enable working men and working women to make their purchases before proceeding to business. On Mondays and Thursdays the pork butchers will close all day, and on Wednesdays and Saturdays the shops will open at 9am. On the four open days serving will go forward till stocks are exhausted; then the shops will close finally for the day. By this means queues waiting for the shops to reopen will disappear.[2]

With beef and pork now in exceedingly short supply, other sources of meat were sometimes substituted. Horseflesh was now offered for sale in Leicester from what were termed 'Belgian Butchers'; the town's medical officer, Dr Killick Millard, was strongly in favour of the use of horsemeat for public consumption, finding it every bit as good as beef. The only restriction placed on establishments selling substitute meat was an 1889 Act of Parliament, which stated that they must display a sign with clearly readable letters stating 'Horseflesh Sold Here'. Winnifred Taylor, a schoolgirl living on Upperton Road in Leicester, remembered many years afterwards:

> We were very short of food ... and the bread was almost black. The meat was rationed, we had coupons of course, and I know that people with a lot of children did better, because they got quite a good ration for the children; I can remember our coupon falling or blowing into the fire and my aunt grabbing it! Anyway it was passed by the butcher alright....but there were a lot of

Policemen keep a watchful eye on a queue outside a pork butchers on Welford Road, Leicester, early in 1918. (Courtesy of the Leicester Mercury)

A slaughterhouse providing horsemeat in Leicester. It was considered an acceptable alternative to beef as meat supplies dwindled. (Record Office)

shortages really. We had to make potato dripping for instance, and my aunt was very good at contriving ... she used to cook this bread in milk for our breakfast because cereals were difficult [to get] but we got through, and I had a friend whose father kept a fruiterers shop and green grocers, so I did well for fruit, but fruit was quite scarce...[3]

Another schoolgirl, Margot Cliff, remembered:

Some of my earliest memories were queuing with mother, before I went to school. I remember once queuing for what seemed like hours for butter at the 'Maypole', only enlivened by watching the assistant pat up slabs of butter into pounds with two wooden patters. Mother was lucky when we moved to Mere Road to find a helpful butcher, Mr Bamford, at the corner of Conduit Street and Sparkenhoe Street. She stuck with him all her life.[4]

However, rationing, with its underlying principle that all people, of whatever class, were equally deserving of the same basic portion of foodstuffs, marked a seismic shift in British society. For so long it had been rigidly stratified, and with a Victorian sense of moral certainty among the upper classes that this was God's way – as the hymn had it, 'the rich man in his castle, the poor man at his gate, God made them high and lowly, and ordered their estate' – even if it meant that the poor were left to starve. A correspondent in the *Leicester Daily Post* in early 1918 even noted that the word 'servant' was going out of use, and had come to be regarded as almost as degrading a term as 'slavery'. Several new synonyms in use included 'household assistants' and 'domestic aids'. The same writer noted that household service was more unpopular than it had ever been (perhaps not surprising when one considers that girls could earn far more money – and respect – in munitions work), but the servants and their role in the household economy were going to be crucial if the war were to be won:

> It might be well if Leicester ladies copied the example of their Sheffield sisters, and arranged a public meeting of domestic servants, to be addressed by some good lady who knows how to talk to these rather sensitive household assistants, and how to put the whole case for rationing before them from the patriotic standpoint. I feel sure that they do not need it more than the rest of us, but it would be nice for them to be made to feel that they, too, are an important body of people, whose aid in winning the war is most important.[5]

In the middle of January 1918, as part of a drive to sell war bonds, the War Office sent a tank (nicknamed 'Ole Bill', after the Bruce Bairnsfather cartoon character) to Leicester to raise public interest. The logistical challenges of moving such a leviathan around the country were not inconsiderable. It arrived from Hanley in Staffordshire, where it had previously been on show, via the Midland Railway; once it had reached the station in Leicester it was unloaded from its truck, and the sponsons and guns were fitted. These side-mounted turrets were removed when transporting tanks by rail, in order to allow them to pass through tunnels. When this was completed, a procession consisting of police, volunteers, a military band, and discharged soldiers and sailors

A cartoon from the Leicester press depicts the monstrous tank as a zoo animal, albeit one which visitors are encouraged to feed.

from the town, led the tank away. It was then driven through the streets of Leicester to the Municipal buildings, the crew negotiating a number of tight corners, whilst the police kept back the mass of people who had turned out to see it.

For a week the tank attracted much attention in Town Hall Square. There was considerable rivalry between Leicester and other towns which had hosted the tank. In particular, Leicester War Savings Committee worthies were anxious that Leicester should surpass the total raised by Birmingham. They need not have worried; by the end of the week an astonishing £2,045,324 had been raised, easily surpassing Birmingham. A number of events took place during the week to publicise the campaign, with speeches from the Mayor, parades and processions, and an appearance by music hall favourite Vesta Tilley. Tuesday, 17 January, was Women's Day. One of the women present, Mrs A.E. Clephan, made a speech in which she stated that she was:

Female porters at work at the Great Central Railway station, Leicester, in 1918. Lucy Lount is the woman on the right. (Record Office)

Glad an especial appeal was being made to the women and hoped they would rise to it. The whole population would have to take part in it, even tiny tots doing their bit. 'Ole Bill' brought an eloquent message to them; it told them of Britain's need of women's help and also of the brave men who were fighting and suffering for the safety of the country. It behoved the women to stop grousing and grumbling and to think of the men who are at the front. They had been used to think of Britain as a safe, rich and comfortable country to live in. At present Britain was still rich, but it could not be said that it was so safe and comfortable, and therefore Britain asked its women to respond in its hour of need by investing as much as possible.[6]

Valuable as they were on the home front in raising money, on the battlefield tanks were only really useful in an offensive to capture ground from the enemy. They could not be used effectively in a defensive role, as the series of heavy blows which fell against the British armies in France in the spring of 1918 would show. The

Germans planned, in a final desperate throw of the dice, to win the war before the Americans could arrive on the battlefield in large numbers. Using tactics honed at Cambrai the previous year, the Germans attacked behind a barrage of gas, their stormtroopers pushing through weak spots in the line and quickly reaching the rear areas, where they over-ran artillery batteries. Strongpoints in the front line, now deprived of artillery support, were left to wither on the vine, and large numbers of British soldiers were captured. The news for local families was again bleak as reports filtered back of loved ones killed or, in many cases, simply recorded as 'missing'.

Sapper Herbert Harrison, of 20 Aylestone Street, Leicester, was a case in point. A member of the 103rd Field Company Royal Engineers, he was captured west of Cambrai on 21 March 1918, and incarcerated at a German PoW camp at Quedlinburg, in the Hartz Mountains. It would be May of that year before his wife received a postcard from him stating that he was alive, the first positive news of her husband in over six weeks. Another Leicester soldier caught up in this maelstrom

Sapper Herbert Harrison, Royal Engineers, of 20 Aylestone Street, Leicester, with his wife and daughter. Captured on 21 March 1918, he was held as a PoW at Quedlinburg, Germany.

was Private William Scroby, from Wharf Street. Serving with the 11th Battalion Cheshire Regiment, he was in the front line when it was over-run. Scroby kept a diary, which remained with him through the months of captivity, and part of it reads:

> March 23 [1918]: Taken prisoner about 4.30pm. Had to carry wounded Germans from the line to a village about five miles away and we were then put in a cage at Inchy.
>
> March 24: Two thousand of us marched to another cage several miles away.
>
> March 25: Left again for another cage and arrived at a big town and put in a school near Denain.
>
> March 26: Still at Denain no work not much grub.
>
> March 29: Left Denain and had to march to a place called Wallers. Billeted in a School.[7]

For a spell Scroby was excused work through an injured foot, but by May he was put to work with other PoWs:

> May 4: Foot nearly better, so I went to work up the line salvaging. Found several useful articles. Weather was grand. Thinking of old Saturday nights drinking etc.
>
> May 5: Day of rest for us. Weather fine. Sent letter to wife and a card to uncle with new address.
>
> May 6: Foot getting better. Went to work up the line salvaging. Weather fine.
>
> May 16: Working up line, pulling down artillery gun-pits and dugouts. Weather glorious.
>
> May 17: Had easy day at work. We were inspected by a big general and had a fine dinner. Weather lovely.
>
> May 18: Working up line, very easy day but weather is awfully

hot. Did some washing after dinner. Thinking of the forthcoming holiday week and wishing I were going to good old Bradgate like the old days.

May 19: Day of rest. Glorious weather. Thinking of good old holiday times. Spent day chiefly in bed.

May 20: Whit Monday. Working on light railway. Weather grand. Sent card to wife. Received first pay for whole of work since capture. 11.40 marks.

May 21: Weather glorious. Went out working up line and found more souvenirs. Had to turn out after tea for instruction in German drill commands.

Private Harry Goodwin, 8th Leicesters. He was aged just 19 when he was killed in action on 27 May 1918. His mother lived at 78 Woodgate, Leicester.

May 22: Had easy day working up line near a German canteen where I bought a jar of jam, a box of cheese, a tin of meat etc. Weather grand.

May 23: Went to Cambrai for a bath. Weather grand but roads very dusty.

May 24: Working on dump near our billet loading up trains. Very hard work and heavy rain all the time.

May 25: Went to work on dump again loading up some motors and some of our captured wagons with old iron and barbed wire. [8]

After the war Scroby wrote up his memories of his time in German captivity, adding much extra detail. He wrote:

[We] managed to make the food spin out by various additions and substitutes such as gathering nettles and dandelions, old cabbage etc. which we were able to gather whilst out working. I had a host of old cooking utensils which I found in the ruined villages we passed through, such as frying pans, saucepans, bowls, and tin mugs and bowls which were all very useful. On returning to our ramshackle billet I used to cook the nettles etc. over a fire in the yard to make a bit of a meal. Another meal was made better by an idea which very soon spread until everyone had caught it. The bread ration was broken up by us into small pieces and put into a pan and boiled in the coffee that we were issued with. This we used to stir over our fire until a thick paste or pudding was made and any jam or meat that we had managed to be issued with was added and made a more appetizing and filling meal than the dry German Black Bread.

We often found useful articles when we were salvaging dugouts and trenches and these were allowed to be kept by us. I found two towels, four handkerchiefs and a shirt and a pair of pants which I washed on a Sunday and made good. Besides the Herbs mentioned, some of the fellows driven by hunger even went to the extent of gathering snails from the trees and cooking them like winkles and any time that a dead horse was found there was always a rush for a slice or two and it was a common sight to see a crowd of them kneeling round one and cutting lumps off which they took to the billet to cook.[9]

Whilst Scroby and other Leicester men were enduring the hardships of German captivity in the wake of the Spring offensives, back home in Leicester a political and ideological battle was to erupt into a physical confrontation, when violent clashes took place at the annual May Day meeting of the supporters and members of the Labour movement. The 1918 event was scheduled for Sunday 5 May, in Leicester market place. That year, however, it would provoke some of the most serious public disorder in Leicester's modern history. Some 6,000 or more people had thronged the market place and most of them, even at this late stage of the war, were still strongly supportive of Britain's stance in the conflict. The main speaker as usual was Ramsay MacDonald, supported by Amos Mann and George Banton. Since the Russian Revolution the previous year, MacDonald had recovered some of the fervour with which he had first vigorously opposed the conflict in 1914. His speech in 1918 was intended to be vehemently anti-war, with fresh calls for a negotiated peace being the central theme. However a combination of ill health, and the raucous heckling of the largely hostile crowd (which at one point began to sing 'God Save the King' in order to drown him out) forced him to cut short his speech. Banton tried to continue in the same vein but at this point fighting broke out in the crowd as a group of soldiers in uniform attempted to force their way through to the platform. Only the intervention of the police restored order. John Riley of the ILP, President of the Trades Councils who had chaired the meeting, recalled afterwards that he never forgot the spectacle of the faces of men and women:

> So distorted almost out of recognition by hatred and passion as on that day.[10]

The violence of the day was attributable not merely to a clash between pro-war and pacifist elements; feelings were further enflamed by the fact that the February 1917 Russian Revolution had widened an already growing split within the Labour movement. Just as MacDonald and the ILP drew heart from the events in Russia and renewed their demands for peace, removal of wartime restrictions and a return to civil liberties, so a rival political organisation emerged to battle for the heart and soul of the British Labour movement. This organisation, which went under a number of names such as the British Workers' League and the National Democratic Labour Party, was a national movement, supportive of the wartime coalition government, and promoted particularly by members of the Social Democratic Federation. In 1917 a branch was established in Leicester. Old campaigners like Joseph Burgess, the first socialist to stand for the borough, came down to speak on its behalf, and J.F. Green, formerly a clergyman and more recently treasurer of the Social Democratic Federation, was adopted as its prospective parliamentary candidate. It was clashes between these rival factions which made the May Day meeting of 1918 such a bitter confrontation. In the longer term, not only would the Labour Party in Leicester emerge from the war discredited by what many regarded as its unpatriotic conduct, but it would also face difficulties in reunifying the working class vote, with a rival party now well established in the town.

In the summer of 1918, however, the people of Leicester perhaps had other concerns, as what would be an eighteen month long influenza pandemic began to take hold. This infamous sickness – which it is said killed more people worldwide than died in the war - came to the town in three main waves: May to August 1918, followed by a further outbreak in the autumn and a third the following winter. A report into the Leicester outbreak by Dr M.B. Arnold makes for interesting reading:

> The staple trades at Leicester are hosiery and boot and shoe making. Visits to two factories, which were said to be typical, showed the following possible means of transference of [disease] particles from one worker to another:
> 1. Roller towels in both factories.
> 2. Enamel drinking cups in one factory.
> 3. Washing of teacups together in one factory.
>
> I was informed that there are canteens in some factories.
>
> Passing of goods in various stages of manufacture from one worker to another. There may be an interval of a day or more between the completion of one process and the beginning of the next, but where there is an urgent demand for one type of finished article, goods may go immediately from one worker to the next.
>   The possibility of droplet infection through the air varies considerably in the various processes. Of those I saw, machining in the shoe factory seemed to offer the greatest opportunity. Workers sit on each side of a long bench and face one another. The distance across the bench is about 5 feet and the lateral distance between the workers about 3 feet …
>   Of women of the age group 15 to 55, 56 per cent went out to work. Amongst those going out to work there were about 34 per cent of attacks and amongst those not going out to work about 30.5 per cent. The difference might easily be accounted for by the fact that the ages in the outworkers group tended to be lower than in the house-worker group.[11]

In spite of the fearsome reputation of the illness, there were, perhaps surprisingly, few fatalities attributed to it. The total number of influenza deaths in the borough between 1918 and 1919 appears to have been around 1600. The group hardest hit by it was that aged between five and thirty-five, these people having both a greater incidence of the illness and a greater mortality rate. Not surprisingly, the report acknowledges that this group had amongst it a high proportion of soldiers, who had begun to return in sizeable numbers either on leave or pending discharge that summer.

Among the latter group was Jack Horner, previously noted as being wounded at the Third Battle of Ypres in 1917, and who had spent part of that year being treated at various hospitals in England and Scotland. In the spring of 1918, he asked to be transferred to Leicester, to be nearer his sweetheart, Sally. His request was granted, and he boarded an overnight train to take him home from Dundee:

> I reached Leicester about 7am. The ambulance was waiting, and we soon reached the Fifth Northern General Hospital … to me a cold forbidding place after the warmth and welcome of St Andrew's hospital at Dundee. I soon made myself at home in the ward, and had my breakfast. The ward was under a Sister with five nurses, all very professional (not at all like the ones I had left at Dundee), who couldn't, or wouldn't, find time for a laugh or a joke – all very cold and austere. As is usual in all hospitals, the doctors' rounds are the main purpose of the mornings. The doctor came at about 10am, and took a good look at my arm, still in the iron stretcher. He told me that I would have to keep it on for some time longer, and went on his way up the ward, with the sister in attendance.[12]

After a spell in a convalescent home near Melton, Horner returned to the hospital to have his wound examined again:

> The following day, the doctor had the bandages taken off. He had a good look at my arm, then took the great iron stretcher splint off which I had been wearing for so long. That in itself was a very great relief. (I also had my first sight of the terrible wound that the jagged piece of metal had done to my arm.) The Doctor stayed with me for quite a while, testing my arm to see how well the bones had knitted. He appeared satisfied on that,

then he asked me to stretch my hand as far as I could – that wasn't at all good. I was asked to grip his hand – very poor. He then measured my left arm against my right, and said arm was three or four inches short, my grip was very weak … Also I should never be able to carry heavy weights, and would never be able to stretch my hand full out, as the main sinews had been badly damaged. He recommended massage twice a day for as long as possible. I thanked him, and through him, all the other doctors, surgeons and nursing staff, whose skill and devoted service had saved my arm from amputation.[13]

After a further period of convalescence at Loughborough, Horner went to North Evington hospital for a final examination by a Medical Officer. This time the doctor was pleased with the progress that he had made, and recommended his discharge from the army. Horner was typical of many hundreds of Leicester ex-soldiers, disabled in the war and now struggling to find a place back in society once more. He wrote afterwards:

Wounded servicemen in the dining hall at the 5th Northern General Hospital.

So, on the 8th August 1918, after bidding goodbye to my comrades, whom I left behind, and to the Sister and her nurses, I left the army as I entered it, by walking down the main drive, carrying all I possessed in a paper parcel, my left arm hanging limply at my side; a bitter battle-scarred veteran, not yet 21, to begin the long walk down the road to the city, where I could get a tramcar for home. Fortunately, a coal-cart came from the hospital boiler room, and was going back to the city. He, the driver, gave me a lift to the main road, where I caught a tram to take me home. What an inglorious end to my war service![14]

He continued:

I was still under treatment, having to go to Victoria Park 5th Northern Hospital for massage every other day, so I called at the Labour Exchange (which was then two huts in Albion Street opposite the *Leicester Mercury* office). The clerks were very helpful. I was told to call every other day, and sign on for £1 a week dole money. I hated and detested having to do it, but there was no alternative – take it or leave it, and I couldn't do that. So with the money I had from the Army Pay Office, I bought a tailor-made suit, cut and made on the premises of 'Deans of Gallowtree Gate', for £6. It was a lovely, well-made suit which lasted me for many years; a pair of boots for 25 shillings together with socks, shirt, tie and underwear, that took about all I had.[15]

Later that year, Horner appeared before a medical board at the hospital, where a panel of doctors assessed his disability at 40%. His pre-war employer, British United Shoe Machinery, gave him his old job back, but with a damaged arm he was unable to undertake work as a fitter in heavy engineering, and had no choice but to leave. He had many jobs in 1918 as he struggled to find a way of making a living, including hawking goods on the market, and chopping and bundling firewood before selling it to shopkeepers. There must have been many others like him, as the wounded drifted back into civilian life with just a suit of clothes and a few shillings war gratuity to help them on their way.

During the course of the summer, Special Service Companies were raised from amongst the Leicester Volunteers to undertake temporary guard duty on the east coast. This allowed the release of regular troops, who were badly needed on the Western Front. The men spent two or three months on this coastal duty, and upon their return the commanding officer Colonel Sarson received an official message of thanks from the War Office. The Volunteers had, it said,

> Enabled the Government to meet a critical situation, and to rise over very difficult days in the history of the war ... up to the limit of their powers they have directly contributed to the improvement of the situation in France, and on more distant fronts.[16]

A Leicester man, probably too old for active service, in the uniform of the Leicester Volunteer Training Corps.

In October 1918 a campaign of protest that had begun in the spring through the pages of Leicester newspapers, came to its conclusion when the German names of several streets were altered to something more English. One letter, from a correspondent who signed himself 'Wounded Discharged', stated:

A football match held at Leicester Fosse's Filbert Street ground, on 28 September 1918, to raise money for Leicester PoWs. The teams are Standard Engineering Co. Ltd vs Legion Works. (Record Office)

Corporal Jabez Thompson, of Leicester (left), a member of the Tank Corps, poses in front of one of his monstrous machines. Tanks would play a significant role in the final Allied offensive of 1918.

Many of us in the town have seen our comrades fall (many blinded) through the effects of liquid fire, and injured by gas attacks, and these [sic], apart from their other crimes, is enough to make us cry out against anything German. You can now help us to wipe out those names which remind us of memories we are trying very hard to forget.[17]

Such was the strength of anti-German feeling at this time that Gotha Street became Gotham Street, Saxe-Coburg Street was renamed Saxby Street and Hanover Street was altered to Andover Street.

On the battlefields of the Western Front that autumn, movement had finally returned, as the Allies now began to drive the exhausted Germans back from the gates of Paris and towards their homeland. Among the British soldiers involved in this campaign was Lance Corporal George Thorpe, a 19-year-old from Leicester who was serving with the Durham Light Infantry. He remembered:

We finally dug in [close] to that River Escault, which runs into the Scheldt eventually, it was canalized, and where we were one side it was all swamp which was lucky because the stuff that came over dug in and flung high. If it had been hard, it would have had a lower trajectory ... they floated a pontoon bridge down there; we got 5 Platoon further down on the enemy's side of the river and they were depending on us in case of a push. ... There was only about 30 men there, they couldn't hold any attack, we'd got to hold this bridge for them and half my platoon were the other side with a Lewis gun, and we covered them both from our side with the other Lewis. It was a hell of a place because [Jerry] was shelling to try to find it, in fact some of the lads got splashed with water from some of these things dropping in the cut...[18]

Thorpe and his men held the position for about four days, until he was taken ill with influenza, which was beginning to sweep through the military as well as civilian populations at this time. He was evacuated to a primitive hospital situated in a factory behind the lines, but the treatment available was rudimentary. Still not fully cured, he was posted back to his unit:

We went back towards Lille ... where I actually saw the news of the Armistice in the little snickett posted up, the news that it had ceased. The night before, we were about four or five miles behind the line, the earth was rocking with them getting shot of the ammunition, both sides, terrific, you could see the fire in the distance as they were exploding in the air, both coming and going ... and then towards the morning it faded off, then at 11 o'clock, absolute silence... we were very relieved, because we were going back towards the battalion.[19]

When the news of the cease fire reached Leicester, there were wild scenes as the civilian population reacted to the sudden release of tension – in marked contrast in fact to the muted response on the Western Front. Winnifred Taylor, a child in Leicester at the time, remembered:

An enormous crowd gathers outside the town hall in Leicester to hear news of the Armistice with Germany, November 1918. (Courtesy of the Leicester Mercury)

[At the end of the war] there was jubilation, absolute jubilation there was. We had all sorts of celebrations … we were very joyful but it was a long while before things got back [to normal].[20]

Margot Cliff was a similar age and also had memories of the excitement which gripped the town:

In the final stages [of the war] we had preparation for air raids. We all had a place. I merely stood in a corner. I envied the children who hid under desks and above all in the cupboard. I remember November 11th 1918 vividly. Teachers just disappeared and later Miss Elmer came in curiously excited and said 'The war's over. You can all go home for the rest of the day'. We all rushed out and children with money rushed to buy a Union Jack from one of the little shops around. We went home and to our surprise, mother gave us 2d but we had to be content

The Leicester Mail *of Monday, 11 November 1918 announces the fact that the Great War is over.*

> with a blue ensign as we were late in the rush … Gwen and I stayed with Arch while mother and dad went to join in the excitement in the town. I distinctly remember going back home on the tram and mother pointing out the Town Hall clock lit up.[21]

In December 1918, Prime Minister David Lloyd George called a general election. It was known as the 'Khaki Election' or 'coupon' election. Every candidate who supported the continuation of the wartime coalition government at Westminster received an endorsement or 'coupon' from Lloyd George, hence the alternative name of 'coupon election'. In Leicester the new constituencies created by the Representation of the People Act (1918), would create severe difficulties for the Liberal Party at this election, and would in turn contribute to its decline nationally. The Act extended the parliamentary borough to include the whole of the municipal borough as it had been enlarged in 1891, and in doing so it brought into it a number of suburban districts, like Stoneygate, which were regarded as generally Unionist (Conservative) in outlook. By dividing the former two-member borough into three single-member constituencies, East Leicester, South Leicester and West Leicester, it also made the traditional tactics by which the Liberals had been able to keep both moderates and Radicals within the same party more difficult. Under the old system, they could be fairly sure of winning both seats, and thus could put up two candidates of different outlooks, both of whom were likely to be returned. Now, with single member constituencies, that compromise was impossible. In addition, the Act increased the total electorate in Leicester to 114,230, of which more than a third were women who had never voted before and thus had no 'tradition' of

Armistice celebrations at Benjamin Russell's hosiery factory.
(Courtesy of Dennis Orme)

Liberal allegiance. A final nail in the Liberal coffin was the disappearance during the war, or in the years immediately following it, of the local, independent Liberal press, which deprived the Liberal Party of an important means of bringing this new electorate under their influence.

The general election of 1918 also reflected the way in which membership of the wartime coalition had weakened the position of the Liberals. In Leicester in particular, the war had also precipitated the breakdown of the local understanding with the Labour Party which the Liberals had had prior to the war. Through this they had allowed MacDonald and Labour a clear run at the second Leicester seat, in order not to split the working class vote. The breaking point for this agreement was the coalition with the Unionists, which the Liberals entered during the course of the war; this was exemplified at a local level when Leicester's Liberal Member of Parliament, Sir Gordon Hewart, accepted the office of Solicitor-General in the coalition government. Of the three coalition candidates put up for Leicester in 1918 only one, Hewart who stood for East Leicester, was a Liberal; the others were a Unionist, T.A. Blane for South Leicester, and for West Leicester, standing as a member of the Patriotic Labour Coalition, J.F. Green of the British Workers' League. So even as part of the war-winning coalition government, the best that the Liberals in Leicester could hope to achieve would be a third and, not as before, a half of the representation.

The coalition candidates faced Labour opponents in each constituency, consisting of Ramsay MacDonald in West Leicester, and in East and South two local men, George Banton and F.F. Riley, both of whom had followed his lead fairly consistently during the war. In Leicester if nowhere else, the election became a referendum on the war record of MacDonald and his Labour associates. The accusations of unpatriotic behaviour made against these three men cost them the support even of some Labour leaders and trades unionists and, as might be expected, all three Labour candidates were severely defeated. In the opinion of one local newspaper, the 'cancer of pacifism' was removed from Leicester by this result, and in its view (probably the view of many, if the election result was anything to go by) the town now stood vindicated before the world.

Epilogue

With the ending of hostilities in 1918 came the abrupt cancellation of many government contracts. Industry, which had been operating at full stretch to meet the demands of war, was forced to apply the brakes harshly, and fears were raised over the economic and social impact that this would have. In Leicester, much of the expected dislocation was avoided as industries wound down from a war footing. Whilst many of the women in Leicester's engineering factories lost their jobs with the coming of peace, in the hosiery industry women in Leicester actually retained much of the ground that they had gained in the workplace during the war. Some of the 'substitutes' were made redundant, but many others were simply re-deployed in other parts of the industry. One Leicester union representative stated:

> Of course women on men's jobs don't like leaving them, or that is generally speaking. Others have said that the machines are too heavy, and they are glad to return to their old ones, but with few exceptions the arrangement [of men returning to the factories] has worked smoothly, and I don't know of one instance but what the women have been found work in some other department.[1]

The Leicester-based National Union of Boot and Shoe Operatives had by the end of 1918 a total membership of 69,000, of whom 20,000 were women. Whilst men and women mixed in most branches, the Leicester Women's Branch, with 4,000 members, formed an important exception. Its president was the one and only woman representative on the executive committee, or on the National Industrial Council for the Boot and Shoe Industry, and remained so in the years which followed.

Some of the many Leicester soldiers who had been decorated for gallantry in the war gather afterwards for a reception at the Guildhall. (Courtesy of Frank Monaghan)

1919 saw the rapid demobilization of the British army, with several million men now facing an uncertain future and a return to civilian life. For many the defeat of Germany had become the guiding tenet of their existence; now that was achieved, what were they to do with their lives? For some the extraordinary circumstances of war had become normality, and it was hard to imagine life without it. Writing in his diary on 28 June 1919, Leicester soldier Edgar Wignall recorded his apprehension and mixed emotion about the prospect of a life full of uncertainty back in the boot and shoe industry:

> At last. After nearly 5 years of active service my demob order has arrived today at dinner time … Expect to leave Charleroi on Thursday for England … It is now 6pm and for some reason I am feeling very depressed. I hope this will soon disappear. It is

His Majesty King George V and Queen Mary visiting the Corah works in Leicester, June 1919 – official recognition of the remarkable contribution that the firm had made to the war effort.

difficult to analyse my feelings. I have [some] feelings of regret at leaving behind the military environment in the midst of which I have lived for the past 5 years. I am leaving behind a beautiful country in which I have enjoyed many hours, and last but not least, some good friends. Looking forwards my prospects do not seem very alluring owing to my industrial position on the outbreak of war.[2]

The same month, Their Majesties King George V and Queen Mary visited Leicester and made a point of inspecting the town's most prominent hosiery manufacturer, Nathanial Corah and Sons. The industries of Leicester had more than pulled their weight during the war years, and none more so than this firm. The Corah works had seen 50% of its male workforce – some 330 men – leave for the war. Whilst they were away, the predominantly female labour force had produced a staggering ten million items of knitwear for government contracts, ranging from socks, cardigans and woollen vests to cotton drawers, scarves, balaclavas and cap comforters. Mrs A. Overton remembered:

Our next door neighbours were a Mr and Mrs Barrows ('Pop' and 'Ma' Barrows, though childless). In 1919 'Pop' took me to see King George V and Queen Mary arrive at the Midland Station on London Road. A kind policeman seeing my bandaged head and leg (yes I was still an outpatient) beckoned us to the front. 'Pop' explained about my war injuries and we had lost Dad in February 1918. Mam was left a widow with seven children under 15 years of age.[3]

Corah's was a particularly paternalistic company, and its historian tells us:

So deep were the feelings of gratitude and relief at the cessation of the 1914-18 war and the prospect of a lasting peace, that Mr and Mrs Alfred Corah decided to entertain the whole of the employees of the firm to a round of festivities at their residence, Scraptoft Hall, near Leicester, on Saturday, 16 August 1919.

The historic hall, lawns, gardens, lake, fields and woods were a perfect picture in the ideal weather of the afternoon, and when all the guests had congregated and distributed themselves to the

Recognition for individual effort during the war, a presentation certificate awarded to a Leicester special constable. Leicester's new status as a city is also proudly acknowledged. (Courtesy of Jim Briggs)

different parts of the estate the scene of animation was extremely charming.

A programme of sports was arranged from 2.30 onwards. The Wigston Silver Prize Band and the Band of the Church Lads Brigade (under the conductorship of Mr Charles Moore) played selections throughout the day.[4]

There was frenzied speculation in Leicester that summer that the visit of His Majesty the King in 1919 would not solely be to visit Corah's, but also to mark the regaining by Leicester of its status as a city (lost many centuries previously) in the wake of the war. In fact, confirmation of this would not come from the Home Secretary until four days after the Royal Visit, but the timing was nonetheless fortunate for Leicester Fosse. The 'Fossils', who had never recovered from the financial difficulties which had bedevilled them before the war, were wound up in May 1919, and a new club was formed in their stead. A fresh lease was negotiated on the Filbert Street ground, and on 5 July the directors gained the consent of the Football League for a change of name that reflected Leicester's elevated status. The new venture was called Leicester City Football Club. The war still cast a long shadow, however, for among the necessary legal papers the new limited company had to file was a declaration under the Trading With The Enemy (Amendment) Act!

Another illustrious institution to emerge in the wake of the conflict was the University of Leicester. Founded in 1921 with nine students, the fledgling college's Fielding Johnson Building was the former Lunatic Asylum (latterly 5th Northern General Hospital). It was so-named because it was a local textile manufacturer, Thomas Fielding Johnson, who gave the land for the university in order to create a living memorial for those who gave their lives in the First World War. This is reflected in the university motto 'Ut Vitam Habeant' – that they might have life. Also among those involved in founding the new University College, as a memorial to those who died in the war was Harry Peach, whose firm Dryad had produced balloon baskets for the War Office. He served on the Board of Governors and was also a major benefactor to the institution. The university gained full degree-awarding powers in 1957, when it was granted its Royal Charter.

The First World War also cast a long shadow in other ways, in Leicester as much as in any other part of Britain. Margot Cliff remembered:

Every Armistice Day until the next war there was a two minutes silence at eleven o'clock. The traffic stopped, people in the street stood still. We had a service at school and stood still when the maroons sounded. Two minutes seemed very long. Mother

The war memorial plaque from Clarendon Park Congregational Church. Woodward, Ockenden, and Lines served with the 1st/4th Leicesters. The latter two prayed together, joined the army together and died together at the Hohenzollern Redoubt.

thought it a stupid idea as it brought everything back to people who had lost someone.

Life changed a lot after the war. Before there was an outlet for the unemployed who could emigrate to the dominions but that was never resumed. So there was a dreadful lot of unemployment. There was also a serious housing shortage as for four years no houses had been built. The returning soldiers didn't come back to 'a land fit for heroes'. [Cousin] Bert found it very difficult to get anywhere to live. Ex-servicemen were forever knocking at the door, with trays of haberdashery. Mother said we must always buy something. Our house can never have been short of tape, elastic or shirt buttons.

Of course the worst thing was the shortage of young men. The girls of that generation, brought up to regard marriage as their natural end often found there was no-one to marry. They had got used to working during the war when factories etc were increasingly manned by women. Hospitals and schools profited from these surplus women. 'A million surplus women' was a catch phrase of the time.

I think a lot of ideas must have changed too. Changes are always hastened by a war. I think people were beginning to doubt the divine right of the upper classes to rule. The Labour Party's rate of growth accelerated and it soon ousted the Liberal Party as the natural opposition. Trades unions grew stronger and improved working conditions and wages. Probably the hold of the churches on ordinary people declined a little. The Victorian confidence in Britain was taking some hard knocks too. Women profited from their war work. The reliance on them to keep the munitions factories going got for them what the suffragettes had failed to do.[5]

Private John T. Atkins, of 55 Kensington Street, Leicester. He sustained a gunshot wound to the chest on 24 March 1918 and was taken as a PoW to Soltau in Germany. He eventually died of war injuries in February 1921, and is buried in Welford Road Cemetery. He left a widow and two children.

Winnifred Taylor remembered:

I started to work in an office … in 1923, that would be five years after the end of the war, and I used to have to answer the little bob hole for enquiries, and there were men who had never had a job in five years, and well-spoken, well-educated men too…[6]

However, in spite of the pressures of war and the hardships which followed in its wake, the working class remained in many ways staunchly un-radicalized by it. Most of the strikes during the war had been about preserving pay and conditions – the traditional preoccupations of the British workman – rather than having political objectives. Lifelong socialist Tom Barclay despaired of the lack of political solidarity among the working class of Leicester in the post-war years, stating:

We have at the present time – November 1924 – several large and well patronized clubs in Leicester: they could, one has to think, be a tremendous influence towards the understanding and solving of social problems, but they are not. I leave the definitely political clubs, such as the Liberal and Constitutional, out of the question, but we have among others the Aylestone, the Belgrave, the Asfordby Street, the Manchester, and the Bond Street, and in not one of these is there such a thing as an educational class, lecture, or debate.[7]

For Barclay, the pity of the post-war working class was that it was too ready to lose itself in idle distractions, rather than working towards socialism, the men spending their days:

…simply thinking of nothing but how to waste the time and to amuse ourselves. Horse-racing, football, sports – these are of

A Leicester war widow: Lilian Dring, of 42 Ash Street, Humberstone Road, who was left with two daughters to bring up alone after her husband was killed in battle in 1918.

Mrs Elizabeth Ann Butler, who lost four sons in the Great War. Together with another bereaved Leicester mother, she was invited to unveil Leicester's war memorial. (Courtesy of Derek Fussell)

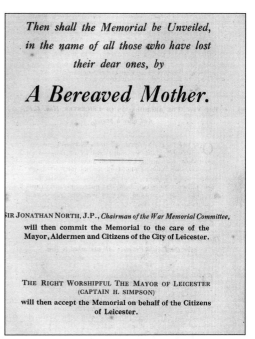

The programme for the unveiling of Leicester's arch of remembrance on Victoria Park, 1925. (Courtesy of Derek Fussell)

primary importance, and we discuss them in and out of factory and workshop, whereas Social Problems are considerably second – or nowhere … Today we have no Labour Club in Leicester; I suppose we've learnt that we'ld [sic] get no proper support of one unless we sold intoxicants, and that if we *did* sell intoxicants there would be little interest in anything else.[8]

In 1925 the war memorial on Victoria Park was unveiled by two women who represented the sacrifice made by the people of Leicester in the Great War. Between them they had lost seven sons in the conflict. One, Mrs Elizabeth Ann Butler, had eight sons, all of whom volunteered to fight and of whom four did not return. The other bereaved mother was Mrs Annie Elizabeth Glover, who lost three of her sons, Arthur, Frank and Harry, in the war. Many ex-soldiers carried with them for the rest of their lives the scars (both mental and physical)

Learning to cope with life-changing injuries: war veteran Walter Malkin of Leicester, a double amputee, seen here at the Chapel Allerton limb centre in Leeds in the 1930s.

Walter Malkin's shop on Tudor Road. The Leicester Corporation helped disabled servicemen to set up such businesses.

of that conflict. In common with that of many other towns, the treatment of Leicester's disabled ex-servicemen often left much to be desired, though efforts were made to help these men retrain and find new lines of work.

Overall, Leicester was a resilient place, its industries remained largely profitable, and in the 1930s it was reckoned to be the second wealthiest city in Europe. Over time the divisions which the First World War had created in society were largely healed; those who had opposed it at the time, such as George Banton, were reconciled with the political establishment (and the electorate). Banton went on to become Mayor of Leicester and subsequently represented one of the Leicester divisions at Westminster. Horace Gladstone Twilley went on to have a successful career in the textile industry; he remained avowedly anti-war, resigning from the ILP in the 1930s because in his view it was not pacifist enough. Sydney Gimson summarized the impact of the war upon the Leicester Secular Society. The membership, both thoughtful and intelligent, was no less divided upon the issues presented by the war than were many other parts of society:

> …some of our members were convinced that the war was inevitable and intended to do all that they could to ensure England's success; a number enlisted at once, others did what was possible at home. Some were lukewarm and did little, others were pacifists and objected to England having entered the war; some went to the length of being 'Conscientious Objectors' and refused to fight when the Government brought in conscription; some suffered imprisonment for their opinions. As a society we tried to be fair to all and respect the many differences of opinion. So far as was possible we would protect all from suffering. As a consequence the society held together, with mutual respect, and we lost few members. I know of one good member who left us because of the "Unpatriotic" talk of some other members, but he was the exception. Most of our members took the view that, being involved in the terrible conflict it was essential to do all in our power to bring it to a successful conclusion for England, though I think all of us recognised that no good was likely to come out of the war.

Sydney Gimson, of the Leicester engineering firm, and his wife. He saw the Great War as a terrible conflict, from which little good was likely to ensue. (Courtesy of Leicester Secular Society)

Gimson's words were prescient, for the Great War did little to resolve the tensions within Europe; nor for long did it suppress German territorial ambitions. Instead it sowed seeds of bitterness and resentment, which would lead to renewed conflict just twenty years later.

Leicester firms engaged in munitions work, 1915–19

Allen, W. & Co.	Great Central Street
Barron, A. & Co.	Rydal Street
Berridge, I.L. & Co.	43 Humberstone Road
Bostock & Co.	Grange Lane
British United Shoe Machinery Co. Ltd	Union Works
Burnell, W.E.	Harvey Lane
Cannon & Stokes	Canning Street
Clarke, T.A.W., Ltd	Havelock Street
Cox, Jane & Co.	York Road
Dale, H.& F.	Oxford Street
Gimson & Co. (Leicester) Ltd	Vulcan Road
Goodwin, Barsby & Co.	Watling Street
Grieve, T. & Co.	Queen Street
Gunton & Co., Ltd	Short Street
Hill & Herbert, Ltd	Great Central Street
Hind, W.H.	Bedford Street
Hollis Patents Machine Co.	Crown Works, Newfoundpool
Jackson, H.E. Ltd	Campbell Street
Jarratt, J.T. & Co.	St Peter's Lane
Jelly & Co.	Oxford Street
Johnson, K. & Sons	Erskine Street
Kennedy-Skipton Co.	Oakland Road
Mellor, Bromley & Co. Ltd	St Saviour's Road East

Midland Counties Motor Garage Co. Ltd — Upper Charles Street
Pegg, S. & Sons — Alexander Street
Pollard, F. & Co. Ltd — St Saviour's Road East
Richards, W. & Sons — Phoenix Iron Works
Russell, S. & Sons — Bath Lane
Spencer, A.T. & Co. — Upper Brown Street
Spiers, William — Walnut Street
Standard Engineering Co. Ltd — Evington Valley Road
Stibbe, G. & Co. — 9/15 Newarke Street
Taylor & Hubbard — Kent Street Works
Taylor, T. & Sons — Gladstone Street
Valley Mills Co. Ltd — Evington Valley Road
Walker, R. & Sons — Abbey Meadow Mills
Wildt & Co., Ltd — The Newarkes
Wilkinson, S.W. & Co — Little Holme Street
Wright's Havelock Foundry Co. Ltd — Havelock Street
Wright, Wallace — Bonners Lane

Military formations based in Leicester upon the outbreak of war, or subsequently raised there

Leicestershire Yeomanry (HQ & B Squadron)
Leicester Royal Horse Artillery (Territorial)
3rd (Special Reserve) battalion Leicestershire Regiment
4th Battalion Leicestershire Regiment (Territorial)
North Midland Company ASC (Territorial)
2nd North Midland Field Ambulance RAMC (Territorial)
Leicester Motor Corps. Raised August 1914
Leicester Volunteer Training Corps. Raised August 1914
6th (Service) Battalion Leicestershire Regiment. Raised August 1914
7th (Service) Battalion Leicestershire Regiment. Raised September 1914
8th (Service) Battalion Leicestershire Regiment. Raised September 1914
9th (Service) Battalion Leicestershire Regiment. Raised September 1914
Leicester Junior Training Corps. Raised November 1914
176th (Leicester) Royal Field Artillery Howitzer brigade. Raised May 1915
11th (Midland Pioneer) Battalion Leicestershire Regiment. Raised October 1915
12th (Reserve) Battalion Leicestershire Regiment. Raised March 1916

Notes

Introduction
1. Ben Beazley, *Leicester During the Great War – Four Years Remembered*, Derby 1999 p 8

Chapter One
1. Francis Armitage *Leicester 1914-18 The War Time Story of a Midland Town* Leicester 1933 p 9
2. *Hansard*, Commons debates 3 August 1914
3. *Leicester Daily Mercury* 27 November 1914
4. Eliot Crawshay-Williams, *Leaves From An Officer's Notebook* London 1918 p 6
5. Alfred Willis, tape recorded interview, author's collection
6. John Milne, *Footprints of the 1/4th Leicestershire Regiment* Leicester 1935 p 3
7. Philip Snow, *Stranger and Brother – A Portrait of C.P. Snow* London 1982 p 5
8. I.L.Read, *Of Those We Loved* Bishop Auckland 1994 p 501
9. Read, *op cit* p 502
10. R.Eric Pochin, *Over My Shoulder and Beyond* Leicester 1971 p 55
11. J.B Pick, *The Pick Knitwear Story 1856-1956* Leicester 1956 p 20
12. *Leicester Mail* 27 November 1914
13. *Leicester Mail* 23 November 1914
14. Sydney Gimson, recollections, courtesy of Leicester Secular Society
15. *Leicester Mail* 2 September 1914
16. East Midlands Oral History Archive, LO/062/013 Sidney Coleman
17. Albert Parr, *A Walk from Leicester to the East Coast* Leicester 1915 p 109
18. *ibid*

19. Pick, *op cit* p 22

20. *Leicester Mail* 28 November 1914

21. Pte George Dodge, typescript diary via Mrs M.Preston

22. *Leicester Mail* 12 December 1914

23. *Leicester Mercury* 2 September 1985

24. *ibid*

25. *Leicester Mail* 6 February 1915

26. *Leicester Daily Mercury* 9 December 1914

27. *Leicester Mail* 6 January 1915

Chapter Two

1. Vera Brittain *Testament of Youth* London 2004 p 101

2. *Leicester Mail* 5 February 1915

3. Charles Bacon, MS88, University of Leicester Special Collections

4. *Leicester Mail* 7 January 1915

5. Denis Dougherty *A South Wigston Lad,* typescript memoir, author's collection

6. *ibid*

7. Jack Horner, typescript memoir, author's collection

8. Armitage, *op cit* p 84

9. Hansard *HC Deb 25 February 1915 vol 70 cc 402-84*

10. Harry Lauder *Between You and Me,* New York 1919 p 176

11. Hansard HC Deb 25 February 1915 vol 70 cc 402-84

12. *Leicester Mercury* 29 August 1915

13. *ibid*

14. East Midlands Oral History Archive LO/078/030 George Draper

15. University of Warwick Modern Records Centre MSS.51/3/1/48. Courtesy of Professor Richard Hyman

16. Tom Barclay *Memoirs and Medleys The Autobiography of a Bottle Washer* Coalville1995 p 57

17. *op cit* p 59

18. *op cit* p 111

19. Leicester ILP *Monthly Notes* No8 July 1915

20. A.Whitehead, (Ed.) *Report of the 47th Annual Co-Operative Congress 1915* Co-Operative Union Ltd, Manchester 1915 p 103

21. Whitehead *op cit* p 109

22. Autograph album of Gladys Forryan. Courtesy of Tony Walne

23. *British Journal of Nursing* 1 May 1915 p 364

24. *ibid*
25. *Leicester Daily Mercury* 8 July 1915
26. Pochin *op cit* pp 55-56
27. Barbara Drake, *Women in Trade Unions,* London 1920 p 133
28. *Leicester War Souvenir* Part II 1915
29. Leicester and District Armaments Group *An Experiment in Engineering Co-Operation 1915 –1918* Leicester 1919
30. *ibid*
31. *Leicester Daily Mercury* 20 October 1915
32. *op cit* 3 November 1915
33. *op cit* 29 October 1915
34. *Leicester Mercury* 25 November 1985
35. http://highfields.dmu.ac.uk/text/THORNLEY.html
36. Autograph album of Gladys Forryan. Courtesy of Tony Walne

Chapter Three
1. Lance Corporal W.Billings, manuscript diary, courtesy of the Billings family.
2. *Leicester Mail* 22 May 1916
3. *Leicester Chronicle* 9 June 1916
4. James Drake, typescript recollections, author's collection
5. Harry Halford, tape recorded interview, author's collection
6. Herbert Orton, tape recorded interview, author's collection
7. Glenn A. Steppler *Britons To Arms!* Stroud 1997 p 124
8. *Leicester Daily Mercury* 21 April 1916
9. Barbara Ann Roberts *A Reconstructed World: A feminist biography of Gertrude Richardson* McGill1996 p 165
10. Roberts *op cit* p 168
11. Roberts *op cit* p 169
12. D.A. Bacon, typescript memoirs. Record Office for Leicester, Leicestershire & Rutland p 60
13. *ibid*
14. *Nottingham Evening News* 18 August 1916
15. Horner *op cit*
16. *Leicester Daily Mercury* 28 September 1916
17. Frank Gayton *Ye Olde Englishe Faire* Leicester 1916
18. Dougherty *op cit*
19. East Midlands Oral History Archive, LO/100/051 Betty Preston

20. Beazley, *op cit* p 114
21. Extract from unpublished notes on her family and early life by Margaret 'Margot' Elaine Cliff (1911-1994) – Gillian Lighton family papers
22. *ibid*
23. Jones & Shipman Christmas 1916 booklet, author's collection
24. *ibid*
25. *ibid*
Chapter Four:
1. Ernest E.Kendall *Doing and Daring the Story of Melbourne Hall Evangelical Free Church Leicester,* Rushden 1955 p 92
2. *ibid*
3. East Midlands Oral History Archive 1206/LO/553/503 Edith Isaac
4. Pochin *op cit* pp 56, 57
5. *Leicester Daily Mercury* 12 May 1917
6. Read *op cit* p 276
7. Read *op cit* p 277
8. Arthur C. Cave, typescript diary, courtesy of Colonel Terry Cave
9. Emma Hancox Soden; letter in the papers of F. Pitts, Liddle Collection, Brotherton Library, University of Leeds
10. Mrs Tutty; letter in the papers of F. Pitts, Liddle Collection, Brotherton Library, University of Leeds
11. Papers of Florence Egerton, Liddle Collection, Brotherton Library, University of Leeds
12. Horner *op cit*
13. Horner *op cit*
14. Letter reproduced in Lyn Macdonald, *They Called it Passchendaele,* London 1978
15. CAB 24/27/102, The National Archives, Kew
16. www.nednewitt.webspace.virginmedia.com/whoswho/R.html
17. Roberts *op cit* p 219

Chapter Five:
1. *Leicester Daily Mercury* 4 February 1918
2. *op cit* 5 February 1918
3. East Midlands Oral History Archive LO/069/020/B Winnifred Taylor
4. Margaret 'Margot' Elaine Cliff *op cit*
5. *Leicester Daily Post* 10 January 1918
6. *op cit* 17 January 1918

7. Typescript diary of William Scroby, courtesy of Ray Scroby
8. *ibid*
9. *ibid*
10. Ned Newitt *A People's History of Leicester* p 98
11. http://influenza.sph.unimelb.edu.au/data/S0001/chapters/app_2.pdf
12. Horner *op cit*
13. *ibid*
14. *ibid*
15. *ibid*
16. Leicestershire Record Office DE819/2 258-9
17. http://www.thisisleicestershire.co.uk/streets-weird-names/story-12054816-detail/story.html#axzz2SpRuDqUE
18. George Thorpe, tape recorded interview, author's collection
19. *ibid*
20. East Midlands Oral History Archive LO/069/020/B Winnifred Taylor
21. Margaret 'Margot' Elaine Cliff *op cit*

Epilogue
1. Barbara Drake *op cit* p 133
2. Edgar Wignall *QMS Edgar Wignall Of The 51st Field Ambulance Royal Army Medical Corps. Diary And Notes From The Great War 1914-1918* Leicester 1999
3. *Leicester Mercury* 2 September 1985
4. C.W.Webb, *Corah's of Leicester* Leicester [sd] p 66
5. Margaret 'Margot' Elaine Cliff *op cit*
6. East Midlands Oral History Archive LO/069/020/B Winnifred Taylor
7. Barclay *op cit* p 63
8. Barclay *op cit* p 64

Bibliography

Armitage, Francis Paul *Leicester 1914–18 The War Time Story of a Midland Town*, Leicester, Edgar Backus, 1933

Barclay, Tom *Memoirs and Medleys The Autobiography of a Bottle Washer,* Coalville, Coalville Publishing Company, 1995

Beazley, Ben *Leicester During the Great War – Four Years Remembered*, Derby, Breedon Books, 1999

Brittain, Vera *Testament of Youth,* London, Virago, 2004

Crawshay-Williams, Eliot *Leaves From an Officer's Notebook,* London, Edward Arnold, 1918

Drake, Barbara *Women in Trade Unions,* London, The Labour Research Department 1920

Gayton, Frank *Ye Olde Englishe Faire* sl sd [Leicester, 1916]

Hopkins, J.R. *Leicester's Great War Hospital: The 5th Northern General Military Hospital, Leicester (1914–19): an Account of the Establishment, Operation and Expansion of the Hospital* sl 1995

Hyman, Richard *The Workers' Union,* Oxford, Clarendon Press 1971

Kendall, Ernest E. *Doing and Daring the Story of Melbourne Hall Evangelical Free Church Leicester,* Rushden, Hunt 1955

Lauder, Harry *Between You and Me,* New York, The James A. McCann Company, 1919

Leicester and District Armaments Group *An Experiment in Engineering Co-Operation 1915–1918,* Leicester, De Montfort Press, 1919

Leicester Oral History Archive *I Remember Leicester: the Great War,* Leicester, 2004

Macdonald, Lyn *They Called It Passchendaele,* London, Michael Joseph Ltd, 1978

Milne, John *Footprints of the 1/4th Leicestershire Regiment,* Leicester, Edgar Backus, 1935

Newett, Ned *A People's History of Leicester,* Derby, Breedon Books, 2008

Parr, Albert *A Walk from Leicester to the East Coast*, Leicester, Gee & Co, 1915

Pick, J.B. *The Pick Knitwear Story 1856–1956,* Leicester, Pick & Sons, 1956

Pochin, R. Eric *Over My Shoulder and Beyond*, Leicester, Goodwin Barsby & Co, 1971

Read, I.L. *Of Those We Loved,* Bishop Auckland, Pentland Press, 1994

Richardson, Matthew *Fighting Tigers,* Barnsley, Pen & Sword Books Ltd, 2002

Richardson, Matthew *The Tigers,* Barnsley, Pen & Sword Books Ltd, 2000

Roberts, Barbara Ann *A Reconstructed World: A feminist biography of Gertrude Richardson,* McGill, Queens University Press, 1996

Smith, Dave and Taylor, Paul *Of Fossils and Foxes,* Leicester, Polar Publishing, 1989

Snow, Philip *Stranger and Brother – A Portrait of C.P. Snow,* London, Macmillan, 1982

Steppler, Glenn A. *Britons To Arms! The Story of the British Volunteer Soldier,* Stroud, Budding Books, 1997

Webb, C.W. *Corah's of Leicester,* Leicester, N.Corah & Sons, [sd]

Whitehead, A. (Ed.) *Report of the 47th Annual Co-Operative Congress 1915* Manchester, Co-Operative Union Ltd, 1915

Wignall, Edgar *QMS Edgar Wignall Of The 51st Field Ambulance Royal Army Medical Corps. Diary And Notes From The Great War 1914–1918,* Leicester, Clive Harrison, 1999

Index